Hunting v

Hunting with the Bow & Arrow

by Saxton T. Pope

I

THE STORY OF THE LAST YANA INDIAN

The glory and romance of archery culminated in England before the discovery of America. There, no doubt, the bow was used to its greatest perfection, and it decided the fate of nations. The crossbow and the matchlock had supplanted the longbow when Columbus sailed for the New World.

It was, therefore, a distinct surprise to the first explorers of America that the natives used the bow and arrow so effectively. In fact, the sword and the horse, combined with the white man's superlative self-assurance, won the contest over the aborigines more than the primitive blunderbuss of the times. The bow and arrow was still more deadly than the gun.

With the gradual extermination of the American Indian, the westward march of civilization, and the improvement in firearms, this contest became more and more unequal, and the bow disappeared from the land. The last primitive Indian archer was discovered in California in the year 1911.

When the white pioneers of California descended through the northern part of that State by the Lassen trail, they met with a tribe of Indians known as the Yana, or Yahi. That is the name they called themselves. Their neighbors called them the Nozi, and the white men called them the Deer Creek or Mill Creek Indians. Different from the other tribes of this territory, the Yana would not submit without a struggle to the white man's conquest of their lands.

The Yana were hunters and warriors. The usual California natives were yellow in color, fat and inclined to be peaceable. The Yana were smaller of stature, lithe, of reddish bronze complexion, and instead of being diggers of roots, they lived by the salmon spear and the bow. Their range extended over an area south of Mount Lassen, east of the Sacramento River, for a distance of fifty miles.

From the earliest settlement of the whites, hostilities existed between them. This resulted in definitely organized expeditions against these Indians, and the annual slaughter of hundreds.

The last big round-up of Mill Creek Indians occurred in 1872, when their tribe was surprised at its seasonal harvest of acorns. Upon this occasion a posse of whites killed such a number of natives that it is said the creek was damned with dead bodies. An accurate account of these days may be obtained from Watterman's paper on the Yana Indians.

During one of the final raids upon the Yana, a little band of Indian women and children hid in a cave. Here they were discovered and murdered in cold blood. One of the white scouting party laconically stated that he used his revolver to blow out their brains because the rifle spattered up the cave too much.

So it came to pass, that from two or three thousand people, the Yana were reduced to less than a dozen who escaped extermination. These were mainly women, old men and children. This tribal remnant sought the refuge of the impenetrable brush and volcanic rocks of Deer Creek Canyon. Here they lived by stealth and cunning. Like wild creatures, they kept from sight until the whites quite forgot their existence.

It became almost a legend that wild Indians lived in the Mount Lassen district. From time to time ranchers or sheep herders reported that their flocks had been molested, that signs of Indians had been found or that arrowheads were discovered in their sheep. But little credence was given these rumors until the year 1908, when an electric power company undertook to run a survey line across Deer Creek Canyon with the object of constructing a dam.

One evening, as a party of linemen stood on a log at the edge of the deep swift stream debating the best place to ford, a naked Indian rose up before them, giving a savage snarl and brandishing a spear. In an instant the survey party disbanded, fell from the log, and crossed the stream in record-breaking time. When they stopped to get their breath, the Indian had disappeared. This was the first appearance of Ishi, the Yana.

Next morning an exploring expedition set out to verify the excited report of the night before. The popular opinion was that no such wildman existed, and that the linemen had been seeing things. One of the group offered to bet that no signs of Indians would be found.

As the explorers reached the slide of volcanic boulders where the apparition of the day before had disappeared, two arrows flew past them. They made a run for the top of the slide and reached it just in time to see two Indians vanish in the brush. They left behind them an old white-haired squaw, whom they had been carrying. She was partially paralyzed, and her legs were bound in swaths of willow bark, seemingly in an effort to strengthen them.

The old squaw was wrinkled with age, her hair was cropped short as a sign of mourning, and she trembled with fear. The white men approached and spoke kindly to her in Spanish. But she seemed not to understand their words, and apparently expected only death, for in the past to meet a white man was to die. They gave her water to drink, and tried to make her call back her companions, but without avail.

Further search disclosed two small brush huts hidden among the laurel trees. So cleverly concealed were these structures that one could pass within a few yards and not discern them. In one of the huts acorns and dried salmon had been stored; the other was their habitation. There was a small hearth for indoor cooking; bows, arrows, fishing tackle, a few aboriginal utensils and a fur robe were found. These were confiscated in the white man's characteristic manner. They then left the place and returned to camp.

Next day the party revisited the site, hoping to find the rest of the
Indians. These, however, had gone forever.

Nothing more was seen or heard of this little band until the year 1911, when on the outskirts of Oroville, some thirty-two miles from the Deer Creek camp, a lone survivor appeared. Early in the morning, brought to bay by a barking dog, huddled in the corner of a corral, was an emaciated naked Indian. So strange was his appearance and so alarmed was the butcher's boy who found him, that a hasty call for the town constable brought out an armed force to capture him.

Confronted with guns, pistols, and handcuffs, the poor man was sick with fear. He was taken to the city jail and locked up for safekeeping. There he awaited death. For years he had believed that to fall into the hands of white men meant death. All his people had been killed by whites; no other result could happen. So he waited in fear and trembling. They brought him food, but he would not eat; water, but he would not drink. They asked him questions, but he could not speak. With the simplicity of the white man, they brought him other Indians of various tribes, thinking that surely all "Diggers" were the same. But their language was as strange to him as Chinese or Greek.

And so they thought him crazy. His hair was burnt short, his feet had never worn shoes, he had small bits of wood in his nose and ears; he neither ate, drank, nor slept. He was indeed wild or insane.

By this time the news of the wild Indian got into the city papers, and Professor T. T. Watterman, of the Department of Anthropology at the University of California, was sent to investigate the case. He journeyed to Oroville and was brought into the presence of this strange Indian. Having knowledge of many native dialects, Dr. Watterman tried one after the other on the prisoner. Through good fortune, some of the Yana vocabulary had been preserved in the records of the University. Venturing upon this lost language, Watterman spoke in Yana the words, *Siwini*, which means pine wood, tapping at the same time the edge of the cot on which they sat.

In wonderment, the Indian's face lighted with faint recognition. Watterman repeated the charm, and like a spell the man changed from a cowering, trembling savage. A furtive smile came across his face. He said in his language, *I nu ma Yaki*—"Are you an Indian?" Watterman assured him that he was.

A great sense of relief entered the situation. Watterman had discovered one of the lost tribes of California; Ishi had discovered a friend.

They clothed him and fed him, and he learned that the white man was good.

Since no formal charges were lodged against the Indian, and he seemed to have no objection, Watterman took him to San Francisco, and there, attached to the Museum of Anthropology, he became a subject of study and lived happily for five years.

From him it was learned that his people were all dead. The old woman seen in the Deer Creek episode was his mother; the old man was his uncle. These died on a long journey to Mt. Lassen, soon after their discovery. Here he had burned their bodies and gone into mourning. The fact that the white men took their means of procuring food, as well as their clothing, contributed, no doubt, to the death of the older people.

Half starved and hopeless, he had wandered into civilization. His father, once the chieftain of the Yana tribe, having domain over all the country immediately south of Mt. Lassen, was long since gone, and with him all his people. Ranchers and stockmen had usurped their country, spoiled the fishing, and driven off the game. The acorn trees of the valleys had been taken from them; nothing remained but evil spirits in the land of his forefathers.

Now, however, he had found kindly people who fed him, clothed him, and taught him the mysteries of civilization. When asked his name, he said: "I have none, because there were no people to name me," meaning that no tribal ceremony had been performed. But the old people had called him Ishi, which means "strong and straight one," for he was the youth of their camp. He had learned to make fire with sticks; he knew the lost art of chipping arrowheads from flint and obsidian; he was the fisherman and the hunter. He knew nothing of our modern life. He had no name for iron, nor cloth, nor horse, nor road. He was as primitive as the aborigines of the pre-Columbian period. In fact, he was a man in the Stone Age. He was absolutely untouched by civilization. In him science had a rare find. He turned back the pages of history countless centuries. And so they studied him, and he studied them.

From him they learned little of his personal history and less of that of his family, because an Indian considers it unbecoming to speak much of his own life, and it brings ill luck to speak of the dead. He could not pronounce the name of his father without calling him from the land of spirits, and this he could only do for some very important reason. But he knew the full history of his tribe and their destruction.

His apparent age was about forty years, yet he undoubtedly was nearer sixty. Because of his simple life he was in physical prime, mentally alert, and strong in body.

He was about five feet eight inches tall, well proportioned, had beautiful hands and unspoiled feet.

His features were less aquiline than those of the Plains Indian, yet strongly marked outlines, high cheek bones, large intelligent eyes, straight black hair, and fine teeth made him good to look upon.

As an artisan he was very skilful and ingenious. Accustomed to primitive tools of stone and bone, he soon learned to use most expertly the knife, file, saw, vise, hammer, ax, and other modern implements.

Although he marveled at many of our inventions and appreciated matches, he took great pride in his ability to make fire with two sticks of buckeye. This he could do in less than two minutes by twirling one on the other.

About this time I became an instructor in surgery at the University Medical School, which is situated next to the Museum. Ishi was employed here in a small way as a janitor to teach him modern industry and the value of money. He was perfectly happy and a great favorite with everybody.

From his earliest experience with our community life he manifested little immunity to disease. He contracted all the epidemic infections with which he was brought in contact. He lived a very hygienic existence, having excellent food and sleeping outdoors, but still he was often sick. Because of this I came in touch with him as his physician in the hospital, and soon learned to admire him for the fine qualities of his nature.

Though very reserved, he was kindly, honest, cleanly, and trustworthy. More than this, he had a superior philosophy of life, and a high moral standard.

By degrees I learned to speak his dialect, and spent many hours in his company. He told us the folk lore of his tribe. More than forty myths or animal stories of his have been recorded and preserved. They are as interesting as the stories of Uncle Remus. The escapades of wildcat, the lion, the grizzly bear, the bluejay, the lizard, and the coyote are as full of excitement and comedy as any fairy story.

He knew the history and use of everything in the outdoor world. He spoke the language of the animals. He taught me to make bows and arrows, how to shoot them, and how to hunt, Indian fashion. He was a wonderful companion in the woods, and many days and nights we journeyed together.

After he had been with us three years we took him back to his own country. But he did not want to stay. He liked the ways of the white man, and his own land was full of the spirits of the departed.

He showed us old forgotten camp sites where past chieftains made their villages. He took us to deer licks and ambushes used by his people long ago. One day in passing the base of a great rock he scratched with his toe and dug up the bones of a bear's paw. Here, in years past, they had killed and roasted a bear. This was the camp of *Ya mo lo ku*. His own camp was called *Wowomopono Tetna* or bear wallow.

We swam the streams together, hunted deer and small game, and at night sat under the stars by the camp fire, where in a simple way we talked of old heroes, the worlds above us, and his theories of the life to come in the land of plenty, where the bounding deer and the mighty bear met the hunter with his strong bow and swift arrows.

I learned to love Ishi as a brother, and he looked upon me as one of his people. He called me *Ku wi*, or Medicine Man; more, perhaps, because I could perform little sleight of hand tricks, than because of my profession.

But, in spite of the fact that he was happy and surrounded by the most advanced material culture, he sickened and died. Unprotected by hereditary or acquired immunity, he contracted tuberculosis and faded away before our eyes. Because he had no natural resistance, he received no benefit from such hygienic measures as serve to arrest the disease in the Caucasian. We did everything possible for him, and nursed him to the painful bitter end.

When his malady was discovered, plans were made to take him back to the mountains whence he came and there have him cared for properly. We hoped that by this return to his natural elements he would recover. But from the inception of his disease he failed so rapidly that he was not strong enough to travel.

Consumed with fever and unable to eat nourishing food, he seemed doomed from the first. After months of misery he suddenly developed a tremendous pulmonary hemorrhage. I was with him at the time, directed his medication, and gently stroked his hand as a small sign of fellowship and sympathy. He did not care for marked demonstrations of any sort.

He was a stoic, unafraid, and died in the faith of his people.

As an Indian should go, so we sent him on his long journey to the land of shadows. By his side we placed his fire sticks, ten pieces of dentalia or Indian money, a small bag of acorn meal, a bit of dried venison, some tobacco, and his bow and arrows.

These were cremated with him and the ashes placed in an earthen jar. On it is inscribed "Ishi, the last Yana Indian, 1916."

And so departed the last wild Indian of America. With him the neolithic epoch terminates. He closes a chapter in history. He looked upon us as sophisticated children—smart, but not wise. We knew many things and much that is false. He knew nature, which is always true. His were the qualities of character that last forever. He was essentially kind; he had courage and self-restraint, and though all had been taken from him, there was no bitterness in his heart. His soul was that of a child, his mind that of a philosopher.

With him there was no word for good-by. He said: "You stay, I go."

He has gone and he hunts with his people. We stay, and he has left us the heritage of the bow.

II

HOW ISHI MADE HIS BOW AND ARROW AND HIS METHODS OF SHOOTING

Although much has been written in history and fiction concerning the archery of the North American Indian, strange to say, very little has been recorded of the methods of manufacture of their weapons, and less in accurate records of their shooting.

It is a great privilege to have lived with an unspoiled aborigine and seen him step by step construct the most perfect type of bow and arrow.

The workmanship of Ishi was by far the best of any Indian in America; compared with thousands of specimens in the museum, his arrows were the most carefully and beautifully made; his bow was the best.

It would take too much time to go into the minute details of his work, and this has all been recorded in anthropologic records, but the outlines of his methods are as follows:

The bow, Ishi called *man-nee*. It was a short, flat piece of mountain juniper backed with sinew. The length was forty-two inches, or, as he measured it, from the horizontally extended hand to the opposite hip. It was broadest at the center of each limb, approximately two inches, and half an inch thick. The cross-section of this part was elliptical. At the center of the bow the handgrip was about an inch and a quarter wide by three-quarters thick, a cross-section being ovoid. At the tips it was curved gently backward and measured at the nocks three-quarters by one-half an inch. The nock itself was square shouldered and terminated in a pin half an inch in diameter and an inch long.

The wood was obtained by splitting a limb from a tree and utilizing the outer layers, including the sap wood. By scraping and rubbing on sandstone, he shaped and finished it. The recurved tips of the bow he made by bending the wood backward over a heated stone. Held in shape by cords and binding to another piece of wood, he let his bow season in a dark, dry place. Here it remained from a few months to years, according to his needs. After being seasoned he backed it with sinew. First he made a glue by boiling salmon skin and applying it to the roughened back of the bow. When it was dry he laid on long strips of deer sinew obtained from the leg tendons. By chewing these tendons and separating their fibers, they became soft and adhesive. Carefully overlapping the ends of the numerous fibers he covered the entire back very thickly. At the nocks he surrounded the wood completely and added a circular binding about the bow.

During the process of drying he bound the sinew tightly to the bow with long, thin strips of willow bark. After several days he removed this bandage and smoothed off the edges of the dry sinew, sized the surface with more glue and rubbed everything smooth with sandstone. Then he bound the handgrip for a space of four inches with a narrow buckskin thong.

In his native state he seems never to have greased his bow nor protected it from moisture, except by his bow case, which was made of the skin from a cougar's tail. But while with us he used shellac to protect the glue and wood. Other savages use buck fat or bear grease.

The bowstring he made of the finer tendons from the deer's shank. These he chewed until soft, then twisted them tightly into a cord having a permanent loop at one end and a buckskin strand at the other. While wet the string was tied between two twigs and rubbed smooth with spittle. Its diameter was one-eighth of an inch, its length about forty-eight inches. When dry the loop was applied to the upper nock of his bow while he bent the bow over his knee and wound the opposite end of the string about the lower nock. The buckskin thong terminating this portion of the string made it easier to tie in several half hitches.

When braced properly the bowstring was about five inches from the belly of the bow. And when not in use and unstrung the upper loop was slipped entirely off the nock, but held from falling away from the bow by a second small loop of buckskin.

Drawn to the full length of an arrow, which was about twenty-six inches, exclusive of the foreshaft, his bow bent in a perfect arc slightly flattened at the handle. Its pull was about forty-five pounds, and it could shoot an arrow about two hundred yards.

This is not the most powerful type of weapon known to Indians, and even Ishi did make stronger bows when he pleased; but this seemed to be the ideal weight for hunting, and it certainly was adequate in his hands.

According to English standards, it was very short; but for hunting in the brush and shooting from crouched postures, it seems better fitted for the work than a longer weapon.

According to Ishi, a bow left strung or standing in an upright position, gets tired and sweats. When not in use it should be lying down; no one should step over it; no child should handle it, and no woman should touch it. This brings bad luck and makes it shoot crooked. To expunge such an influence it is necessary to wash the bow in sand and water.

In his judgment, a good bow made a musical note when strung and the string is tapped with the arrow. This was man's first harp, the great grandfather of the pianoforte.

By placing one end of his bow at the corner of his open mouth and tapping the string with an arrow, the Yana could make sweet music. It sounded like an Aeolian harp. To this accompaniment Ishi sang a folk-song telling of a great warrior whose bow was so strong that, dipping his arrow first in fire, then in the ocean, he shot at the sun. As swift as the wind, his arrow flew straight in the round open door of the sun and put out its light. Darkness fell upon the earth and men shivered with cold. To prevent themselves from freezing they grew feathers, and thus our brothers, the birds, were born.

Ishi called an arrow *sa wa*.

In making arrows the first thing is to get the shafts. Ishi used many woods, but he preferred witch hazel. The long, straight stems of this shrub he cut in lengths of thirty-two inches, having a diameter of three-eighths of an inch at the base when peeled of bark.

He bound a number of these together and put them away in a shady place to dry. After a week or more, preferably several months, he selected the best shafts and straightened them. This he accomplished by holding the concave surface near a small heap of hot embers and when warm he either pressed his great toe on the opposite side, or he bent the wood backward on the base of the thumb. Squinting down its axis he lined up the uneven contours one after the other and laid the shaft aside until a series of five was completed. He made up arrows in lots of five or ten, according to the requirements, his fingers being the measure.

The sticks thus straightened he ran back and forth between two grooved pieces of sandstone or revolved them on his thigh while holding the stones in his hand, until they were smooth and reduced to a diameter of about five-sixteenths of an inch. Next they were cut into lengths of approximately twenty-six inches. The larger end was now bound with a buckskin thong and drilled out for the depth of an inch and a half to receive the end of the foreshaft. He drilled this hole by fixing a long, sharp bone in the ground between his great toes and revolved the upright shaft between his palms on this fixed point, the buckskin binding keeping the wood from splitting.

The foreshaft was made of heavier wood, frequently mountain mahogany. It was the same diameter as the arrow, only tapering a trifle toward the front end, and usually was about six inches long. This was carefully shaped into a spindle at the larger end and set in the recently drilled hole of the shaft, using glue or resin for this purpose. The joint was bound with chewed sinew, set in glue.

The length of an arrow, over all, was estimated by Ishi in this manner. He placed one end on the top of his breast-bone and held the other end out in his extended left hand. Where it touched the tip of his forefinger it was cut as the proper length. This was about thirty-two inches.

The rear end of his arrow was now notched to receive the bowstring. He filed it with a bit of obsidian, or later on, with three hacksaw blades bound together until he made a groove one-eighth of an inch wide by three-eighths deep. The opposite end of the shaft was notched in a similar way to receive the head. The direction of this latter cut was such that when the arrow was on the bow the edge of the arrowhead was perpendicular, for the fancied reason that in this position the arrow when shot enters between the ribs of an animal more readily. He did not seem to recognize that an arrow rotates.

At this stage he painted his shafts. The pigments used in the wilds were red cinnabar, black pigment from the eye of trout, a green vegetable dye from wild onions, and a blue obtained, he said, from the root of a plant. These were mixed with the sap or resin of trees and applied with a little stick or hairs from a fox's tail drawn through a quill.

His usual design was a series of alternating rings of green and black starting two inches from the rear end and running four inches up the shaft. Or he made small circular dots and snaky lines running down the shaft for a similar distance. When with us he used dry colors mixed with shellac, which he preferred to oil paints because they dried quicker. The painted area, intended for the feathers, is called the shaftment and not only helps in finding lost arrows, but identifies the owner. This entire portion he usually smeared with thin glue or sizing.

A number of shafts having been similarly prepared, the Indian was ready to feather them. A feather he called *pu nee*. In fledging arrows Ishi used eagle, buzzard, hawk or flicker feathers. Owl feathers Indians seem to avoid, thinking they bring bad luck. By preference he took them from the wings, but did not hesitate to use tail feathers if reduced to it. With us he used turkey pinions.

Grasping one between the heel of his two palms he carefully separated the bristles at the tip of the feather with his fingers and pulled them apart, splitting the quill its entire length. This is called stripping a feather. Taking the wider half he firmly held one end on a rock with his great toe, and the other end between the thumb and forefinger of his left hand. With a piece of obsidian, or later on a knife blade, he scraped away the pith until the rib was thin and flat.

Having prepared a sufficient number in this way he gathered them in groups of three, all from similar wings, tied them with a bit of string and dropped them in a vessel of water. When thoroughly wet and limp they were ready for use.

While he chewed up a strand of sinew eight or ten inches long, he picked up a group of feathers, stripped off the water, removed one, and after testing its strength, folded the last two inches of bristles down on the rib, and the rest he ruffled backward, thus leaving a free space for later binding. He prepared all three like this.

Picking up an arrow shaft he clamped it between his left arm and chest, holding the rear end above the shaftment in his left hand. Twirling it slowly in this position, he applied one end of the sinew near the nock, fixing it by overlapping. The first movements were accomplished while holding one extremity of the sinew in his teeth; later, having applied the feathers to the stick, he shifted the sinew to the grasp of the right thumb and forefinger.

One by one he laid the feathers in position, binding down the last two inches of stem and the wet barbs together. The first feather he applied on a line perpendicular to the plane of the nock; the two others were equidistant from this. For the space of an inch he lapped the sinew about the feathers and arrow-shaft, slowly rotating it all the while, at last smoothing the binding with his thumb nail.

The rear ends having been lashed in position, the arrow was set aside to dry while the rest were prepared.

Five or ten having reached this stage and the binding being dry and secure, he took one again between his left arm and chest, and with his right hand drew all the feathers straight and taut, down the shaft. Here he held them with the fingers of his left hand. Having marked a similar place on each arrow where the sinew was to go, he cut the bristles off the rib. At this point he started binding with another piece of wet sinew. After a few turns he drew the feathers taut again and cut them, leaving about a half inch of rib. This he bound down completely to the arrow-shaft and finished all by smoothing the wet lapping with his thumb nail.

The space between the rib and the wood he sometimes smeared with more glue to cause the feather to adhere to the shaft, but this was not the usual custom with him. After all was dry and firm, Ishi took the arrow and beat it gently across his palm so that the feathers spread out nicely.

As a rule the length of his feathers was four inches, though on ceremonial arrows they often were as long as eight inches.

After drying, the feathers were cut with a sharp piece of obsidian, using a straight stick as a guide and laying the arrow on a flat piece of wood. When with us he trimmed them with scissors, making a straight cut from the full width of the feather in back, to the height of a quarter of an inch at the forward extremity. On his arrows he left the natural curve of the feather at the nock, and while the rear binding started an inch or more from the butt of the arrow, the feather drooped over the nock. This gave a pretty effect and seemed to add to the steering qualities of the missile.

Two kinds of points were used on Ishi's arrows. One was the simple blunt end of the shaft bound with sinew used for killing small game and practice shots. The other was his hunting head, made of flint or obsidian. He preferred the latter.

Obsidian was used as money among the natives of California. A boulder of this volcanic glass was packed from some mountainous districts and pieces were cracked off and exchanged for dried fish, venison, or weapons. It was a medium of barter. Although all men were more or less expert in flaking arrowheads and knives, the better grades of bows, arrows, and arrow points were made by the older, more expert specialists of the tribe.

Ishi often referred to one old Indian, named *Chu no wa yahi*, who lived at the base of a great cliff with his crazy wife. This man owned an ax, and thus was famous for his possessions as well as his skill as a maker of bows. From a distant mountain crest one day Ishi pointed out to me the camp of this Indian who was long since dead. If ever Ishi wished to refer to a hero of the bow, or having been beaten in a shot, he always told us what *Chu no wa yahi* could have done.

To make arrowheads properly one should smear his face with mud and sit out in the hot sun in a quiet secluded spot. The mud is a precaution against harm from the flying chips of glass, possibly also a good luck ritual. If by chance a bit of glass should fly in the eye, Ishi's method of surgical relief was to hold his lower lid wide open with one finger while he slapped himself violently on the head with the other hand. I am inclined to ascribe the process of removal more to the hydraulic effect of the tears thus started than to the mechanical jar of the treatment.

He began this work by taking one chunk of obsidian and throwing it against another; several small pieces were thus shattered off. One of these, approximately three inches long, two inches wide and half an inch thick, was selected as suitable for an arrowhead, or *haka*. Protecting the palm of his left hand by a piece of thick buckskin, Ishi placed a piece of obsidian flat upon it, holding it firmly with his fingers folded over it.

In his right hand he held a short stick on the end of which was lashed a sharp piece of deer horn. Grasping the horn firmly while the longer extremity lay beneath his forearm, he pressed the point of the horn against the edge of the obsidian. Without jar or blow, a flake of glass flew off, as large as a fish scale. Repeating this process at various spots on the intended head, turning it from side to side, first reducing one face, then the other, he soon had a symmetrical point. In half an hour he could make the most graceful and perfectly proportioned arrowhead imaginable. The little notches fashioned to hold the sinew binding below the barbs he shaped with a smaller piece of bone, while the arrowhead was held on the ball of his thumb.

Flint, plate glass, old bottle glass, onyx—all could be worked with equal facility. Beautiful heads were fashioned from blue bottles and beer bottles.

The general size of these points was two inches for length, seven-eighths for width, and one-eighth for thickness. Larger heads were used for war and smaller ones for shooting bears.

Such a head, of course, was easily broken if the archer missed his shot. This made him very careful about the whole affair of shooting.

When ready for use, these heads were set on the end of the shaft with heated resin and bound in place with sinew which encircled the end of the arrow and crossed diagonally through the barb notches with many recurrences.

Such a point has better cutting qualities in animal tissue than has steel. The latter is, of course, more durable. After entering civilization, Ishi preferred to use iron or steel blades of the same general shape, or having a short tang for insertion in the arrowhead.

Ishi carried anywhere from five to sixty arrows in a quiver made of otter skin which hung suspended by a loop of buckskin over his left shoulder.

His method of bracing or stringing the bow was as follows: Grasping it with his right hand at its center, with the belly toward him, and the lower end on his right thigh, he held the upper end with his left hand while the loop of the string rested between his finger and thumb. By pressing downward at the handle and pulling upward with the left hand he so sprung the bow that the loop of the cord could be slipped over the upper nock.

In nocking his arrow, the bow was held diagonally across the body, its upper end pointing to the left. It was held lightly in the palm of the left hand so that it rested loosely in the notch of the thumb while the fingers partially surrounded the handle. Taking an arrow from his quiver, he laid it across the bow on its right side where it lay between the extended fingers of his left hand. He gently slid the arrow forward until the nock slipped over the string at its center. Here he set it properly in place and put his right thumb under the string, hooked upward ready to pull. At the same time he flexed his forefinger against the side of the arrow, and the second finger was placed on the thumb nail to strengthen the pull.

Thus he accomplished what is known as the Mongolian release.

Only a few nations ever used this type of arrow release, and the Yana seem to have been the only American natives to do so.

To draw his bow he extended his left arm. At the same time he pulled his right hand toward him. The bow arm was almost in front of him, while his right hand drew to the top of his breast bone. With both eyes open he sighted along his shaft and estimated the elevation according to the distance to be shot.

He released firmly and without change of position until the arrow hit. He preferred to shoot kneeling or squatting, for this was most favorable for getting game.

His shooting distances were from ten yards up to fifty. Past this range he did not think one should shoot, but sought rather to approach his game more closely.

In his native state he practiced shooting at little oak balls, or bundles of grass bound to represent rabbits, or little hoops of willow rolled along the ground. Like all other archers, if Ishi missed a shot he always had a good excuse. There was too much wind, or the arrow was crooked, or the bow had lost its cast, or, as a last resource, the coyote doctor bewitched him, which is the same thing we mean when we say it is just bad luck. While with us he shot at the regulation straw target, and he is the first and only Indian of whose shooting any accurate records have been made.

Many exaggerated reports exist concerning the accuracy of the shooting of American Indians; but here we have one who shot ever since childhood, who lived by hunting, and must have been as good, if not better, than the average.

He taught us to shoot Indian style at first, but later we learned the old English methods and found them superior to the Indian. At the end of three months' practice, Dr. J. V. Cooke and I could shoot as well as Ishi at targets, but he could surpass us at game shooting.

Ishi never thought very much of our long bows. He always said, "Too much *man-nee*." And he always insisted that arrows should be painted red and green.

But when we began beating him at targets, he took all his shafts home and scraped the paint off them, putting back rings of blue and yellow, doubtless to change his luck. In spite of our apparent superiority at some forms of shooting, he never changed his methods to meet competition. We, of course, did not want him to.

Small objects the size of a quail the Indian could hit with regularity up to twenty yards. And I have seen him kill ground squirrels at forty yards; yet at the same distances he might miss a four-foot target. He explained this by saying that the target was too large and the bright colored rings diverted the attention. He was right.

There is a regular system of shooting in archery competition. In America there is what is known as the American Round, which consists of shooting thirty arrows at each of the following distances: sixty, fifty, and forty yards. The bull's-eye on the target is a trifle over nine inches and is surrounded by four rings of half this diameter. Their value is 9, 7, 5, 3, 1, successively counting from the center outward. The target itself is constructed of straw, bound in the form of a mat four feet in diameter, covered with a canvas facing.

Counting the hits and scores on the various distances, a good archer will make the following record. Here is Arthur Young's best score:

March 25, 1917.
At 60 yards 30 hits 190 score 11 golds
50 yards 30 hits 198 score 9 golds
40 yards 30 hits 238 score 17 golds
Total 90 hits 626 score 37 golds
This is one of the best scores made by American archers.
Ishi's best record is as follows:

October 23, 1914.
At 60 yards 10 hits 32 score 50 yards 20 hits 92 score 2 golds 40 yards 19 hits 99 score 2 golds
Total 49 hits 223 score 4 golds
His next best score was this:
At 60 yards 13 hits 51 score
50 yards 17 hits 59 score
40 yards 22 hits 95 score
Total 52 hits 205 score
My own best practice American round is as follows:
May 22, 1917.
At 60 yards 29 hits 157 score
50 yards 29 hits 185 score
40 yards 30 hits 196 score
Total 88 hits 538 score
Anything over 500 is considered good shooting.

It will be seen from this that the Indian was not a good target shot, but in field shooting and getting game, probably he could excel the white man.

III

ISHI'S METHODS OF HUNTING

Hunting with Ishi was pure joy. Bow in hand, he seemed to be transformed into a being light as air and as silent as falling snow. From the very first we went on little expeditions into the country where, without appearing to instruct, he was my teacher in the old, old art of the chase. I followed him into a new system of getting game. We shot rabbits, quail, and squirrels with the bow. His methods here were not so well defined as in the approach to larger game, but I was struck from the first by his noiseless step, his slow movements, his use of cover. These little animals are flushed by sound and sight, not scent. Another prominent feature of Ishi's work in the field was his indefatigable persistence. He never gave up when he knew a rabbit was in a clump of brush. Time meant nothing to him; he simply stayed until he got his game. He would watch a squirrel hole for an hour if necessary, but he always got the squirrel.

He made great use of the game call. We all know of duck and turkey calls, but when he told me that he lured rabbits, tree squirrels, wildcats, coyote, and bear to him, I thought he was romancing. Going along the trail, he would stop and say, "*Ineja teway—bjum—metchi bi wi,*" or "This is good rabbit ground." Then crouching behind a suitable bush as a blind, he would place the fingers of his right hand against his lips and, going through the act of kissing, he produced a plaintive squeak similar to that given by a rabbit caught by a hawk or in mortal distress. This he repeated with heartrending appeals until suddenly one or two or sometimes three rabbits appeared in the opening. They came from distances of a hundred yards or more, hopped forward, stopped and listened, hopped again, listened, and ultimately came within ten or fifteen yards while Ishi dragged out his squeak in a most pathetic manner. Then he would shoot.

To test his ability one afternoon while hunting deer, I asked the Yana to try his call in twelve separate locations. From these twelve calls we had five jackrabbits and one wildcat approach us. The cat came out of the forest, cautiously stepped nearer and sat upon a log in a bright open space not more than fifty yards away while I shot three arrows at him, one after the other; the last clipped him between the ears.

This call being a cry of distress, rabbits and squirrels come with the idea of protecting their young. They run around in a circle, stamp their feet, and make great demonstrations of anger, probably as much to attract the attention of the supposed predatory beast and decoy him away, as anything else.

The cat, the coyote, and the bear come for no such humane motive; they are thinking of food, of joining the feast.

I learned the call myself, not perfectly, but well enough to bring squirrels down from the topmost branches of tall pines, to have foxes and lynx approach me, and to get rabbits.

Not only could Ishi call the animals, but he understood their language. Often when we have been hunting he has stopped and said, "The squirrel is scolding a fox." At first I said to him, "I don't believe you." Then he would say, "Wait! Look!" Hiding behind a tree or rock or bush, in a few minutes we would see a fox trot across the open forest.

It seemed that for a hawk or cat or man, the squirrel has a different call, such that Ishi could say without seeing, what molested his little brother.

Often have we stopped and rested because, so he said, a bluejay called far and wide, "Here comes a man!" There was no use going farther, the animals all knew of our presence. Only a white hunter would advance under these circumstances.

Ishi could smell deer, cougar, and foxes like an animal, and often discovered them first this way. He could imitate the call of quail to such an extent that he spoke a half-dozen sentences to them. He knew the crow of the cock on sentinel duty when he signals to others; he knew the cry of warning, and the run-to-shelter cry of the hen; her command to her little ones to fly; and the "lie low" cluck; then at last the "all's well" chirp.

Deer he could call in the fawn season by placing a folded leaf between his lips and sucking vigorously. This made a bleat such as a lamb gives, or a boy makes blowing on a blade of grass between his thumbs.

He also enticed deer by means of a stuffed buck's head which he wore as a cap, and bobbing up and down behind bushes excited their curiosity until they approached within bow-shot. Ordinarily in hunting deer, the Indian used what is termed the still hunt, but with him it was more than that. First of all he studied the country for its formation of hills, ridges, valleys, canyons, brush and timber. He observed the direction of the prevailing winds, the position of the sun at daybreak and evening. He noted the water holes, game trails, "buck look-outs," deer beds, the nature of the feeding grounds, the stage of the moon, the presence of salt licks, and many other features of importance. If possible, he located the hiding-place of the old bucks in daytime, all of which every careful hunter does. Next, he observed the habits of game, and the presence or absence of predatory beasts that kill deer.

Having decided these and other questions, he prepared for the hunt. He would eat no fish the day before the hunt, and smoke no tobacco, for these odors are detected a great way off. He rose early, bathed in the creek, rubbed himself with the aromatic leaves of yerba buena, washed out his mouth, drank water, but ate no food. Dressed in a loin cloth, but without shirt, leggings or moccasins, he set out, bow and quiver at his side. He said that clothing made too much noise in the brush, and naturally one is more cautious in his movements when reminded by his sensitive hide that he is touching a sharp twig.

From the very edge of camp, until he returned, he was on the alert for game, and the one obvious element of his mental attitude was that he suspected game everywhere. He saw a hundred objects that looked like deer, to every live animal in reality. He took it for granted that ten deer see you where you see one—so see it first! On the trail, it was a crime to speak. His warning note was a soft, low whistle or a hiss. As he walked, he placed every footfall with precise care; the most stealthy step I ever saw; he was used to it; lived by it. For every step he looked twice. When going over a rise of ground he either stooped, crawled or let just his eyes go over the top, then stopped and gazed a long time for the slightest moving twig or spot of color. Of course, he always hunted up wind, unless he were cutting across country or intended to flush game.

At sunrise and sunset he tried always to get between the sun and his game. He drifted between the trees like a shadow, expectant and nerved for immediate action.

Some Indians, covering their heads with tall grass, can creep up on deer in the open, and rising suddenly to a kneeling posture shoot at a distance of ten or fifteen yards. But Ishi never tried this before me. Having located his quarry, he either shot, at suitable ranges, or made a detour to wait the passing of the game or to approach it from a more favorable direction. He never used dogs in hunting.

When a number of people hunted together, Ishi would hide behind a blind at the side of a deer trail and let the others run the deer past. In his country we saw old piles of rock covered with lichen and moss that were less than twenty yards from well-marked deer trails. For numberless years Indians had used these as blinds to secure camp meat.

In the same necessity, the Indian would lie in wait near licks or springs to get his food; but he never killed wantonly.

Although Ishi took me on many deer hunts and we had several shots at deer, owing to the distance or the fall of the ground or obstructing trees, we registered nothing better than encouraging misses. He was undoubtedly hampered by the presence of a novice, and unduly hastened by the white man's lack of time. His early death prevented our ultimate achievement in this matter, so it was only after he had gone to the Happy Hunting Grounds that I, profiting by his teachings, killed my first deer with the bow.

That he had shot many deer, even since boyhood, there was no doubt. To prove that he could shoot through one with his arrows, I had him discharge several at a buck killed by our packer. Shooting at forty yards, one arrow went through the chest wall, half its length; another struck the spine and fractured it, both being mortal wounds.

It was the custom of his tribe to hunt until noon, when by that time they usually had several deer, obtained, as a rule, by the ambush method. Having pre-arranged the matter, the women appeared on the scene, cut up the meat, cooked part of it, principally the liver and heart, and they had a feast on the spot. The rest was taken to camp and made into jerky.

In skinning animals, the Indian used an obsidian knife held in his hand by a piece of buckskin. I found this cut better than the average hunting knife sold to sportsmen. Often in skinning rabbits he would make a small hole in the skin over the abdomen and blow into this, stripping the integument free from the body and inflating it like a football, except at the legs.

In skinning the tail of an animal, he used a split stick to strip it down, and did it so dextrously that it was a revelation of how easy this otherwise difficult process may be when one knows how. He tanned his skins in the way customary with most savages: clean skinning, brain emulsion, and plenty of elbow grease.

His people killed bear with the bow and arrow. Ishi made a distinction between grizzly bear, which he called *tet na*, and black bear, which he called *bo he*. The former had long claws, could not climb trees, and feared nothing. He was to be let alone. The other was "all same pig." The black bear, when found, was surrounded by a dozen or more Indians who built fires, and discharging their arrows at his open mouth, attempted to kill him. If he charged, a burning brand was snatched from the fire and thrust in his face while the others shot him from the side. Thus they wore him down and at last vanquished him.

In his youth, Ishi killed a cinnamon bear single handed. Finding it asleep on a ledge of rock, he sneaked close to it and gave a loud whistle. The bear rose up on its hind legs and Ishi shot him through the chest. With a roar the bear fell off the ledge and the Indian jumped after him. With a short-handled obsidian spear he thrust him through the heart. The skin of this bear now hangs in the Museum of Anthropology in mute testimony of the courage and daring of Ishi. Had this young man been given a name, perhaps they would have called him Yellow Bear.

While he shot many birds, I never saw Ishi try wing shooting except at eagles or hawks. For these he would use an arrow on which he had smeared mud to make it dark in color. A light shaft is readily discerned by these birds, and I have often seen them dodge an arrow. But the darker one is almost invisible head on. The feathers of the arrows were close cropped to make them swift and noiseless.

The sound of a bowstring is that of a sharp twang accompanied by a muffled crack. To avoid this and make a silent shot, the Indian bound his bow at the nocks with weasel fur; this effectually damped the vibration of the string, while the passage of the arrow across the bow, which gives the slight crack, is abolished by a heavy padding of buckskin at this point.

Ishi never wore an arm guard or glove or finger stalls to protect himself as other archers do. He seemed not to need them. When he released the arrow, the bow rotated in his hand so that the string faced in the opposite direction from which it started. His thumb alone drew the string, and this was so toughened that it needed no leather covering.

In a little bag he carried extra arrowheads and sinews, so that in a pinch he could mend his arrows.

When not actually in use, he promptly unstrung his bow, and gently straightened it by hand. In cold weather he heated it over a fire before bracing it. The slightest moisture would deter him from shooting, unless absolutely necessary—he was so jealous of his tackle. If his bowstring stretched in the heat or dampness, as sinew is liable to do, he shortened it by twisting one end prior to bracing it.

Before shooting he invariably looked over each arrow, straightened it in his hands or by his teeth, re-arranged its feathers, and saw that the point was properly adjusted. In fact, he gave infinite attention to detail. With him, every shot must count. Besides arrows in his quiver, he carried several ready for use under his right arm, which he kept close to his side while drawing the bow.

In all things pertaining to the handicraft of archery and the technique of shooting, he was most exacting. Neatness about his tackle, care of his equipment, deliberation and form in his shooting were typical of him; in fact, he loved his bow as he did no other of his possessions. It was his constant companion in life and he took it with him on his last long journey.

IV

ARCHERY IN GENERAL

Our experience with Ishi waked the love of archery in us, that impulse which lies dormant in the heart of every Anglo-Saxon. For it is a strange thing that all the men who have centered about this renaissance in shooting the bow, in our immediate locality, are of English ancestry. Their names betray them. Many have come and watched and shot a little, and gone away; but these have stayed to hunt.

From shooting the bow Indian fashion, I turned to the study of its history, and soon found that the English were its greatest masters. In them archery reached its high tide; after them its glory passed.

But the earliest evidence of the use of the bow is found in the existence of arrowheads assigned to the third interglacial period, nearly 50,000 years ago.

That man had material culture prior to this epoch, there is no doubt, and the use of the bow with arrows of less complicated structure must have preceded this period.

All races and nations at one time or another have used the bow. Even the Australian aborigine, who is supposed to have been too low in mental development to have understood the principles of archery, used a miniature bow and poisoned arrow in shooting game. In the magnificent collection of Joseph Jessop of San Diego, California, I saw one of these little bows scarcely more than a foot long. The arrows, he stated, the natives carried in the hair of their heads.

Those who are interested in the archaeology of the bow should read the volume on archery of the Badminton Library by Longmans.

Various peoples have excelled in shooting, notably the Japanese, the Turks, the Scythians, and the English. Others have not been suited by temperament to use the bow. The Latins, the Peruvians, and the Irish seem never to have been toxophilites. The famous long bow of Merrie Old England was brought there by the Normans, who inherited it from the Norsemen settled along the Rhine. Here grew the best yew trees in days gone by, and this, doubtless, was a strong determining factor in the superior development of their archery.

Before the battle of Hastings, the Saxons used the short, weak weapon common to all primitive people. The conquered Saxon, deprived of all arms such as the boar-spear, the sword, the ax, and the dagger, naturally turned to the bow because he could make this himself, and he copied the Norman long bow.

Although the first game preserves in England were established by William the Conqueror at this time, the Saxon was permitted to shoot birds and small beasts in his fields and therefore was allowed to use a blunt arrow, headed with a lead tip or pilum, hence our term pile, or target point. If found with a sharp arrowhead, the so-called broadhead used for killing the king's deer, he was promptly hanged. The evidence against such a poacher was summed up thus in the old legend:

Dog draw, stable stand
Back berond, bloody hand.

One found following a questing hound, posed in the stand of an archer, carrying game on his back, or with the evidence of recent butchery on his hands, was hanged to the nearest tree by his own bowstring.

It was under these circumstances that outlawry took the form of deer killing and robust archery became the national sport. In these days the legendary hero, the demi-myth, Robin Hood, was born. What boy has not thrilled at the tales of Greenwood men, the well-sped shaft, the arrow's low whispering flight, and the willow wand split at a hundred paces?

Every boy goes through a period of barbarism, just as the nations have passed, and during that age he is stirred by the call of the bow. I, too, shot the toy bows of boyhood; shot with Indian youths in the Army posts of Texas and Arizona. We played the impromptu pageants of Robin Hood, manufactured our own tackle, and carried it about with unfailing fidelity; hunted small birds and rabbits, and were the usual savages of that age.

But when it comes to the legends of the bow, the records of these past glories are so vague that we must accept them as a tale oft told; it grows with the telling.

It seems that distances were measured in feet, paces, yards, or rods with blithe indifference, and the narrator added to them at will. Robin is supposed to have shot a mile, and his bow was so long and so strong no man could draw it. In sooth, he was a mighty hero, and yet the ballads refer to him as a "slight fellow," even "a bag of bones." As a youth he slew the king's deer at three hundred yards, a right goodly shot! And no doubt it was.

Of all the bows of the days when archery was in flower, only two remain. These are unfinished staves found in the ship *Mary Rose*, sunk off the coast of Albion in 1545. This vessel having been raised from the bottom of the ocean in 1841, the staves were recovered and are now in the Tower of London. They are six feet, four and three-quarters inches long, one and one-half inches across the handle, one and one-quarter inches thick, and proportionately large throughout. The dimensions are recorded in Badminton. Of course, they never have been tested for strength, but it has been estimated at 100 pounds.

Determined to duplicate these old bows, I selected a very fine grained stave of seasoned yew and made an exact duplicate, according to the recorded measurements.

This bow, when drawn the standard arrow length of twenty-eight inches, weighed sixty-five pounds and shot a light flight arrow two hundred and twenty-five yards. When drawn thirty-six inches, it weighed seventy-six pounds and shot a flight arrow two hundred and fifty-six yards. From this it would seem that even though these ancient staves appear to be almost too powerful for a modern man to draw, they not only are well within our command, but do not shoot a mile.

The greatest distance shot by a modern archer was made by Ingo Simon, using a Turkish composite bow, in France in 1913. The measured distance was four hundred and fifty-nine yards and eight inches. That is very near the limit of this type of bow and far beyond the possibilities of the yew long bow. But the long bow is capable of shooting heavier shafts and shooting them harder.

Since archery is fast disappearing from the land, and the material for study will soon become extinct, I have undertaken to record the strength and shooting qualities of a representative number of the available bows in preservation, together with the power of penetration of arrows.

To do this, through the mediation of the Department of Anthropology of the University of California, I have had access to the best collection of bows in America. Thousands of weapons were at my disposal in various museums, and from these I selected the best preserved and strongest to shoot.

The formal report of these experiments is in the publications of the University, and here 'tis only necessary to mention a few of the findings.

In testing the function of these bows and their ability to shoot, a bamboo flight arrow made by Ishi was used as the standard. It was thirty inches long, weighed three hundred and ten grains, and had very low cropped feathers. It carried universally better than all other arrows tested, and flew twenty per cent farther than the best English flight arrows.

To make sure that no element of personal weakness entered into the test, I had these bows shot by Mr. Compton, a very powerful man and one used to the bow for thirty years. I myself could draw them all, and checked up the results.

It is axiomatic that the weight and the cast of a bow are criteria of its value as a weapon in war or in the chase. Weight, as used by an archer, means the pull of a bow when full drawn, recorded in pounds.

The following is a partial list of those weighed and shot. They are, of course, all genuine bows and represent the strongest. Each was shot at least six times over a carefully measured course and the greatest flight recorded. All flights were made at an elevation of forty-five degrees and the greatest possible draw was given each shot. In fact we spared no bows because of their age, and consequently broke two in the testing.

	Weight	Distance Shot
Alaskan	80 pounds	180 yards
Apache	28 "	120 "
Blackfoot	45 "	145 "
Cheyenne	65 "	156 "
Cree	38 "	150 "
Esquimaux	80 "	200 "
Hupa	40 "	148 "
Luiseno	48 "	125 "
Navajo	45 "	150 "
Mojave	40 "	110 "
Osage	40 "	92 "
Sioux	45 "	165 "
Tomawata	40 "	148 "
Yurok	30 "	140 "
Yukon	60 "	125 "

Yaki......................... 70 " 210 "
Yana......................... 48 " 205 "

The list of foreign bows is as follows:

	Weight	Distance Shot
Paraguay	60 pounds	170 yards
Polynesian	49 "	172 "
Nigrito	56 "	176 "
Andaman Islands	45 "	142 "
Japanese	48 "	175 "
Africa	54 "	107 "
Tartar	98 "	175 "
South American	50 "	98 "
Igorrote	26 "	100 "
Solomon Islands	56 "	148 "
English target bow (imported)	48 "	220 "
English yew flight bow	65 "	300 "
Old English hunting bow	75 "	250 "

It will be seen from these tests that no existing aboriginal bow is very powerful when compared with those in use in the days of robust archery in old England.

The greatest disappointment was in the Tartar bow which was brought expressly from Shansi, China, by my brother, Col. B. H. Pope. With this powerful weapon I expected to shoot a quarter of a mile; but with all its dreadful strength, its cast was slow and cumbersome. The arrow that came with it, a miniature javelin thirty-eight inches long, could only be projected one hundred and ten yards. In making these shots both hands and feet were used to draw the bow. A special flight arrow thirty-six inches long was used in the test, but with hardly any increase of distance gained.

After much experimenting and research into the literature, I constructed two horn composite bows, such as were used by the Turks and Egyptians. They were perfect in action, the larger one weighing eighty-five pounds. With this I hoped to establish a record, but after many attempts my best flight was two hundred and ninety-one yards. This weapon, being only four feet long, would make an excellent buffalo bow to be used on horseback.

In shooting for distance, of course, a very light missile is used, and nothing but empirical tests can determine the shape, size, and weight that suits each bow. Consequently, we use hundreds of arrows to find the best. For more than seven years these experiments have continued, and at this stage of our progress the best flight arrow is made of Japanese bamboo five-sixteenths of an inch in diameter, having a foreshaft of birch the same diameter and four inches long. The nock is a boxwood plug inserted in the rear end, both joints being bound with silk floss and shellacked. The point is the copper nickel jacket of the present U. S. Army rifle bullet, of conical shape. The feathers are parabolic, three-quarters of an inch long by one-quarter high, three in number, set one inch from the end, and come from the wing of an owl. The whole arrow is thirty inches long, weighs three hundred and twenty grains, and is very rigid.

With this I have shot three hundred and one yards with a moderate wind at my back, using a Paraguay ironwood bow five feet two inches long, backed with hickory and weighing sixty pounds. This is my best flight shot.

It is not advisable here to go further into this subject; let it stand that the English yew long bow is the highest type of artillery in the world.

Although the composite Turkish bows can shoot the farthest, it is only with very light arrows; they are incapable of projecting heavier shafts to the extent of the yew long bow, that is, they can transmit velocity but not momentum; they have resiliency, but not power.

Besides these experiments with bows, many tests were made of the flight and penetration of arrows. A few of the pertinent observations are here noted.

A light arrow from a heavy bow, say a sixty-five pound yew bow, travels at an initial velocity of one hundred and fifty feet per second, as determined by a stopwatch.

Shooting at one hundred yards, such an arrow is discharged at an angle of eight degrees, and describes a parabola twelve to fifteen feet high at its crest. Its time in transit is of approximately two and one-fifth seconds.

Shooting straight up, such an arrow goes about three hundred and fifty feet high, and requires eight seconds for the round trip. This test was made by shooting arrows over very tall sequoia trees, of known height.

The striking force of a one-ounce arrow shot from a seventy-five pound bow at ten yards, is twenty-five foot pounds. This test is made by shooting at a cake of paraffin and comparing the penetration with that made by falling weights. Such a striking force is, of course, insignificant when compared with that of a modern bullet, viz., three thousand foot pounds. Yet the damage done by an arrow armed with a sharp steel broad-head is often greater than that done by a bullet, as we shall see later on.

A standard English target arrow rotates during flight six complete revolutions every twenty yards, or approximately fifteen times a second. Heavy hunting shafts turn more slowly. This was ascertained by shooting two arrows at once from the same bow, their shafts being connected by a silk thread, so that one paid off as the other wound up the thread. The number of complete loops, of course, indicated the number of revolutions. A sand-bank makes a good butt to catch them. In rotating, much depends on the size and shape of the feather.

Shooting a blunt arrow from a seventy-five pound bow at a white pine board an inch thick, the shaft will often go completely through it. A broad hunting head will penetrate two or three inches, then bind. But the broad-head will go through animal tissue better, even cutting bones in two; in fact, such an arrow will go completely through any animal but a pachyderm.

To test a steel bodkin pointed arrow such as was used at the battle of Cressy, I borrowed a shirt of chain armor from the Museum, a beautiful specimen made in Damascus in the 15th Century. It weighed twenty-five pounds and was in perfect condition. One of the attendants in the Museum offered to put it on and allow me to shoot at him. Fortunately, I declined his proffered services and put it on a wooden box, padded with burlap to represent clothing.

Indoors at a distance of seven yards, I discharged an arrow at it with such force that sparks flew from the links of steel as from a forge. The bodkin point and shaft went through the thickest portion of the back, penetrated an inch of wood and bulged out the opposite side of the armor shirt. The attendant turned a pale green. An arrow of this type can be shot about two hundred yards, and would be deadly up to the full limit of its flight.

The question of the cutting qualities of the obsidian head as compared to those of the sharpened steel head, was answered in the following experiment:

A box was so constructed that two opposite sides were formed by fresh deer skin tacked in place. The interior of the box was filled with bovine liver. This represented animal tissue minus the bones.

At a distance of ten yards I discharged an obsidian-pointed arrow and a steel-pointed arrow from a weak bow. The two missiles were alike in size, weight, and feathering, in fact, were made by Ishi, only one had the native head and the other his modern substitute. Upon repeated trials, the steel-headed arrow uniformly penetrated a distance of twenty-two inches from the front surface of the box, while the obsidian uniformly penetrated thirty inches, or eight inches farther, approximately 25 per cent better penetration. This advantage is undoubtedly due to the concoidal edge of the flaked glass operating upon the same principle that fluted-edged bread and bandage knives cut better than ordinary knives.

In the same way we discovered that steel broad-heads sharpened by filing have a better meat-cutting edge than when ground on a stone.

In our experience with game shooting, we never could see the advantage of longitudinal grooves running down the shaft of the arrow, such as some aborigines use, supposed to promote bleeding. In the first place these marks are inadequate in depth, and secondly it is not the exterior bleeding that kills the wounded animal so much as the internal hemorrhage.

A sufficiently wide head on the arrow cuts a hole large enough to permit the escape of excess blood, and, as a matter of fact, nearly all of our shots are perforating, going completely through the body.

Conical, blunt, and bodkin points lack the power of penetration in animal tissue inherent in broad-heads; correspondingly they do less damage.

Catlin, in his book on the North American Indian, relates that the Mandans, among other tribes, practiced shooting a number of arrows in succession with such dexterity that their best archer could keep eight arrows up in the air at one time.

Will Thompson, the dean of American archery, writing in *Forest and Stream* of March, 1915, says very definitely that the feat of the legendary hero, Hiawatha, who is supposed to have shot so strong and far that he could shoot the tenth arrow before the first descended, is manifestly absurd. Thompson contends that no man ever has, or ever will keep more than three arrows up in the air at once.

Having read this and determined to try the experiment of dextrous shooting, I constructed a dozen light arrows having wide nocks and flattened rear ends so they might be fingered quickly. Then I devised a way of grasping a supply of ready shafts in the bow hand, and invented an arrow release in which all the fingers and thumb held the arrow on the string, yet remained entirely on the right side of it.

After quite a bit of practice in accurate, later in rapid, nocking, I succeeded in shooting seven successive arrows in the air before the first touched the ground. I used a perpendicular flight. Upon several occasions I almost accomplished eight at once. I feel that with considerable practice eight, and even more, are possible, proving again that there is an element of truth in all legends.

It has long been a bone of contention among archers which element of the yew, the sap wood or the heart, gives the greater cast. To obtain experimental evidence, I constructed two miniature bows, each twenty-two inches long, one of pure white sap wood, the other of the heart from the same stave. I made them the same size, and weighing about eight pounds when drawn eight inches.

Shooting a little arrow on these bows, the sap wood shot forty-three yards; the red wood sixty-six yards, showing the greater cast to be in the red yew.

Corroborating this, Mr. Compton relates that while working in Barnes's shop in Forest Grove, Oregon, during the last illness of that noted bowyer, he came across a laminated bow made entirely of sap wood. Barnes stated that he had constructed it at the instigation of Will Thompson. The cast of this bow was slow, flabby, and weak. As a shooting implement it was a failure.

Taking two pieces of wood, one white and one red, each twelve inches long, I placed them in a bench vise and fastened a spring scale to the top of each. Drawing the sap wood four inches from the perpendicular, it pulled eight pounds. Drawing the heart wood the same distance it pulled fourteen pounds, showing the greater strength of the latter. When drawn five inches from a straight line, the red piece broke. The sap wood could be bent at a right angle without fracture.

It is obvious from this that the sap wood excels in tensile strength the red wood in compression strength and resiliency. In fact, they are reciprocal in action. The red yew on the belly of the bow gives the energy, the sap wood preserves it from fracture. It is, in fact, equivalent to sinew backing, and though less durable, probably adds more to the cast of the bows.

In our experiments with a catgut and rawhide backing, we have not found that they add materially to the cast of a bow, only insure it against fracture. On the other hand, sap wood and hickory backing materially add to the power of the implement.

The little red yew bow used in the previous experiment was backed heavily with rawhide and catgut. It then weighed ten pounds, but only shot sixty-three yards, showing a decrease in cast. But the backing permitted its being drawn to ten inches, when it shot a distance of eighty-five yards. A draw of twelve inches fractured it across the handle.

In a similar experiment it was shown that two pieces of wood of the same size, but one being of a coarse-grained yew running sixteen lines to the inch, the other a fine-grained piece running thirty-five lines to the inch, the finer grain had the greater strength and resiliency up to the breaking point, but the yellow coarse-grained piece was more flexible and less readily broken.

The question often arises, "How would an arrow fly if the bow is held in a mechanical rest and the string released by a mechanical release?" Such an apparatus would permit of several experiments. It would answer some of the queries that naturally pass through the mind of every archer.

Question 1. How accurate is the bow and arrow as a weapon of precision, or as they say in ballistics, "What is the error of dispersion?"

Question 2. What is the angle of declination to the left of the point of aim in the flight of such an arrow?

Question 3. What is the effect of placing the cock feather next the bow?

Question 4. What is the effect of shooting different arrows? How do they group? Would not such a machine give accurate data regarding the flight of new arrows and help in the selection of shafts for target shooting?

Question 5. What effect does the time of holding a bow full drawn have on the flight of an arrow?

Question 6. What is the result of changing the weight of bows when the arrows remain the same?

Therefore, we devised a rest, consisting of a post set firmly in the ground, with a rigid cross arm and a vise-like hand grip. This latter was padded thickly with rubber, so that some resiliency was permitted. The bow was fastened in this mechanical hand by sturdy set screws.

At the other end of the cross arm a hinged block was attached, from which projected two short wooden fingers, serving the exact function of the drawing hand. These were spaced so that the arrow nock fitted between them, and when the string was pulled into position and caught upon these fingers, the bow was drawn 28 inches.

We adopted a system of loading, drawing and releasing on count, so that every shot was delivered with equal time factors.

Answer 1. Using the same arrow each time, with the target set at 60 yards, we found, of course, that the arrow always flies to the left when drawn on the left side of the bow, and that the angle of divergence for a 50 pound bow and a 5 shilling English target arrow was between six and seven degrees. Using a stronger bow this angle was increased,—also that with a weaker arrow the angle was greater,—but six degrees might be designated as the normal declination.

Answer 2. Every rifle expert knows what his gun is capable of, in accuracy, and an archer should know just what to expect of an arrow under the most favorable conditions. We therefore tried shooting the same arrow over the same course with the same release, under these fairly stable conditions: The day was calm. We shot an arrow ten times in succession and all the shots centered in a six inch bull's-eye; that is, none went out of a circle of this diameter. In other words, at sixty yards a bow can shoot arrows with an error of dispersion of no more than six inches. This is surprisingly accurate for a weapon of this sort, when it is considered that the best rifles of today will average between one and a half to three inches dispersion at 100 yards.

Answer 3. Placing the cock feather next the bow diverts the arrow to the left and causes it to drop lower on the target. The group formed by six flights was fairly close and consistent.

Answer 4. Out of nine arrows tested, five consistently made a good close group and four as consistently went out. The "outs," however, were uniform in the direction and distance they took. It would be possible by this machine to select arrows that would make co-incidental patterns. It is obvious, however, that differences in individual arrows are greatly exaggerated by the apparatus, because it was quite apparent by this test that any good archer could group these hits much closer than the machine delivered them.

Answer 5. In our shooting, we universally allotted five seconds for drawing, setting and discharging. However, when this time was increased to fifteen seconds, we found that our groups averaged seven and one-half inches lower. This shows the decided loss of cast incidental to long holding of the bow.

Answer 6. Placing a 65 pound bow in the frame immediately showed increased reactions throughout. The lateral divergence in arrow flight was increased to fifteen degrees and all individual reactions were correspondingly increased. The flight of the individual arrow was less consistent, showing plainly the necessity of a proper relation in weight between the arrow and bow,—a very essential factor in accurate shooting.

In conclusion, it seems to me that the machine naturally exaggerated the errors, for this reason. If the pressure of the arrow against the bow, in passing, amounts to two ounces, the arrow will fly a two ounce equivalent to the left, when the bow is held rigidly. An arrow that exerts four ounces pressure will fly correspondingly a greater distance to the left. But when the bow is held in the hand, there is considerable give to the muscles and the two ounce pressure is compensated for; thus, the arrow tends to fly straight. The four ounce arrow would with the same adjustment hold a correspondingly straighter course.

The vertical error, however, depends more on the weight of the arrow, on the feathering, the holding time, the maintainance of tension, and on the release of the bowstring.

There are many problems in the ballistics of archery that are unsolved, waiting the experiments of modern science. Empirical methods have dictated the art so far. In target equipment and shooting there is a wide field for investigation. Our interests, however, are more those of the hunter, and less those of the physicist.

V

HOW TO MAKE A BOW

Every field archer should make his own tackle. If he cannot make and repair it, he will never shoot very long, because it is in constant need of repair.

Target bows and arrows may be bought in sporting stores, here or in England, but hunting equipment must be made. Moreover, when a man manufactures his bow and arrows, he appreciates them more. But it will take many attempts before even the most mechanically gifted can expect to produce good artillery. After having made more than a hundred yew bows, I still feel that I am a novice. The beginner may expect his first two or three will be failures, but after that he can at least shoot them.

Since there are so many different kinds of bows and all so inferior to the English longbow, we shall describe this alone.

Yew wood is the greatest bow timber in the world. That was proved thousands of years ago by experience. It is indeed a magic wood!

But yew wood is hard to get and hard to make into a bow once having got it. Nevertheless, I am going to tell you where you can get it and how to work it, and how to make hunting bows just as we use them today, and presumably just as our forefathers used them before us. Later on I shall tell you what substitutes may be used for yew.

The best yew wood in America grows in the Cascade Mountains of Oregon, in the Sierra Nevada and Coast Ranges of northern California. By addressing the Department of Forestry, doubtless one can get in communication with some one who will cut him a stave. Living in California, I cut my own.

A description of yew trees and their location may be had from Sudworth's "*Forest Trees of the Pacific Slope*," to be obtained from the Government Printing Office at Washington.

My own staves I cut near Branscomb, Mendocino County, and at Grizzly Creek on the Van Duzen River, Humboldt County, California. Splendid staves have been shipped to me from this latter county, coming from the neighborhood of Korbel.

Yew is an evergreen tree with a leaf looking a great deal like that of redwood, hemlock, or fir at a distance. It is found growing in the mountains, down narrow canyons, and along streams. It likes shade, water, and altitude. Its bark is reddish beneath and scaly or fuzzy on the surface. Its limbs stand straight out from the trunk at an acute angle, not drooping as those of the redwood and fir.

The sexes are separate in yew. The female tree has a bright red gelatinous berry in autumn, and the male a minute cone. It is interesting that in bear countries the female trees often have long wounds in the bark, or deep scratches made by the claws of these animals as they climb to get the yew berries. It is also stated by some authorities that the female yew has light yellow wood, is coarser grained, and does not make so good a bow. I have tried to verify this, but so far I have found some of my bear marked female yew to be the better staves.

The best wood is, of course, dark and close grained. This generally exists in trees that have one side decayed. It seems that the rot stains the rest of the wood and nature makes the grain more compact to compensate for the loss of structural strength. It is also apparent that yew grown at high altitudes, over three thousand feet, is superior to lowland yew.

In selecting a tree for a hunting bow, the stave must be at least six feet long, free from limbs, knots, twists, pitch pockets, rot, small sprouting twigs and corrugations. One will look over a hundred trees to find one good bow stave; then he may find a half dozen excellent staves in one tree.

There is no such thing as a perfect piece of yew, nor is there a perfect bow; at least, I have never seen it. But there is a bow in every yew tree if we but know how to get it out. That is the mystery of bowmaking. It takes an artist, not an artisan.

Before one ever fells a tree, he should weigh the moral right to do so. But yew trees are a gift from the gods, and grown only for bows. If you are sure you see one good bow in a tree, cut it. Having felled it and marked with your eye the best stave, cut it again so that your stave is seven feet long. Then split the trunk into halves or quarters with steel or wooden wedges so that your stave is from three to six inches wide. Cut out the heart wood so that the billet is about three inches thick. Be careful not to bruise the bark in any of these operations.

Now put your stave in the shade. If you are compelled to ship it by express, wrap it in burlap or canvas, and preferably saw the ends square and paint them to prevent checking. When you get it home put it in the cellar.

If you must make a bow right away, place the stave in running water for a month, then dry in a shady place for a month, and it is ready for use. It will not be so good as if seasoned three to seven years, but it will shoot; in fact, it will shoot the same day you cut it from the tree, only it will follow the string and not stand straight as it should. Of course, it will not have the cast of air-seasoned wood.

The old authorities say, cut your yew in the winter when the sap is down, or as Barnes, the famous bow-maker of Forest Grove, Oregon, used to say: "Yew cut in the summer contains the seeds of death." But this does not seem to have proved the case in my experience. I am fully convinced that the sap can be washed out and the process of seasoning hastened very materially by proper treatment.

Kiln dried wood is never good as a bow. It is too brash; but after the first month of shade, the staves may be put in a hot attic to their advantage.

In selecting the portion of the tree best suited for a bow, choose that part that when cut will cause the stave to bend backward toward the bark. Since your bow ultimately will bend in the opposite direction, this natural curve tends to form a straighter bow, or as an archer would say "set back a bit in the handle."

If it is impossible to get a stave six feet in length, then a wide stave three and a half feet long may be used. It is necessary in this case to split it and join the two pieces with a fishtail splice in the handle. Target bows are made this way, to advantage, but such a makeshift is to be deprecated in a hunting bow. The variations of temperature and moisture combined with hard usage in hunting demand a solid, single stave. It must not break. Your life may depend upon it.

Before engaging in any art, it is necessary to study the anatomy of your subject. The anatomical points of a bow have a time-honored nomenclature and are as follows: Bows may be single staves, or one-piece bows, those of one continuity and homogeneity; spliced bows consist of two pieces of wood united in the handle; backed bows have an added strip of wood glued on the back; and composite bows are made up of several different substances, such as wood, horn, sinew, and glue.

That surface of the bow which faces the string when drawn into action, that is, the concave arc, is called the belly of the bow. The opposite surface is the back. A bow should never be bent backwards, away from the belly; it will break.

The center of the bow is the handle or hand grip; the extremities are the tips, usually finished with notches cut in the wood or surmounted by horn, bone, sinew, wooden or metal caps called nocks. These are grooved to accommodate the string. The spaces between the nocks and the handle are called the limbs.

A bow that when unstrung bends back past the straight line is termed reflexed. One that continues to bend toward the belly is said to follow the string. A lateral deviation is called a cast in the bow.

The proper length of a yew bow should be the height of the man that shoots it, or a trifle less. Our hunting bows are from five feet six inches to five feet eight inches in length. The weight of a hunting bow should be from fifty to eighty pounds. One should start shooting with a bow not over fifty pounds, and preferably under that. At the end of a season's shooting he can command a bow of sixty pounds if he is a strong man. Our average bows pull seventy-five pounds. Though it is possible for some of us to shoot an eighty-five pound bow, such a weapon is not under proper control for constant use.

Some pieces of yew will make a stronger bow at given dimensions than others. The finer the grain and the greater the specific gravity, the more resilient and active the wood, and stronger the bow.

Taking a yew stave having a dark red color and a layer of white sap wood about a quarter of an inch thick, covered with a thin maroon-colored bark, let us make a bow. Counting the rings in the wood at the upper end of the stave, you will find that they run over forty to the inch.

Ishi insisted that this end of the stave should always be the upper end of the weapon. It seems to me that this extremity having the most compact grain, and the strongest, should constitute the lower limb, because, as we shall see later on, this limb is shorter, bears the greater strain, and is the one that gives down the sooner.

We shall plan to make the bow as strong as is compatible with good shooting, and reduce its strength later to meet our requirements.

Look over the stave and estimate whether it is capable of yielding two bows instead of one. If it be over three inches wide, and straight throughout, then rip it down the center with a saw. Place one stave in a bench vise and carefully clean off the bark with a draw knife. Do not cut the sap wood in this process.

Cut your stave to six feet in length. Sight down it and see how the plane of the back twists. If it is fairly consistent, draw a straight line down the center of the sap wood. This is the back of your bow. Now draw on the back an outline which has a width of an inch and a quarter extending for a distance of a foot above and a foot below the center. Let this outline taper in a gentle curve to the extremities of the bow, where it has a width of three-quarters of an inch. This will serve as a rough working plan and is sufficiently large to insure that you will get a strong weapon.

With the draw knife, and later a jack plane, cut the lateral surfaces down to this outline. The back must stand a tremendous tensile strain and the grain of the wood should not be injured in any way. But you may smooth it off very judiciously with a spoke shave, and later with a file. The transverse contour of this part of the bow remains as it was in the tree, a long flat arc.

Shift the stave in the vise so that the sap wood is downward, and set it so that the average plane of the sap is level. With the raw knife shave the wood very carefully, avoiding cutting too deeply or splitting off fragments, until the bow assumes the thickness of one and one-quarter inches in the center and this decreases as it approaches the tips, where it is half an inch thick.

The shape of a cross-section of the belly of the bow should be a full Roman arch. Many debates have centered on the shape of this part of the weapon. Some contend for a high-crested contour, or Gothic arch, what is termed "stacking a bow"; some have chosen a very flat curve as the best. The former makes for a quick, lively cast and may be desirable in a target implement, but it is liable to fracture; the latter makes a soft, pleasant, durable bow, but one that follows the string. Choose the happy medium.

The process of shaping the belly is the most delicate and requires more skill than all the rest. In the first place you must follow the grain of the wood. If the back twists and undulates, your cut must do the same. The feather of the grain must never be reversed, but descend by perfect gradation from handle to tip.

Where a knot or pin occurs in the wood, here you must leave more substance because this is a weak spot. If the pin be large and you cannot avoid it, then it is best to drill it out carefully and fill the cavity with a solid piece of hard wood set in with glue. A pin crumbles while an inserted piece will stand the strain. If such a "Dutchman" be not too large nor too near the center of either limb, it will not materially jeopardize the bow. If, in your shaving, you come across a sharp dip in' the grain, such that will make a decided concavity, here leave a few more layers of grain than you would were the contour even; for a concave structure cannot stand strain as well as a straight one; the leverage is increased unduly.

The following measurements, with a caliper, are those of my favorite hunting bow, called "Old Horrible," and with which I've slain many a beast. The width just above the handle is 1-1/4 by 1-1/8 inches thick. Six inches up the limb the width is 1-1/4, thickness 11-1/16.

Twelve inches above the handle it is a trifle less than 1-1/4 wide by 1 inch thick. Eighteen inches above the handle it is 1-1/8 wide by 7/8 thick. Twenty-four inches above it is 15/16 wide by 3/4 thick. Thirty inches above it is 11/16 by 9/16 thick. At the nock it is practically 1/2 by 1/2 inches.

Having got the bow down to rough proportions, the next thing is to cut two temporary nocks on it, very near the ends. These consist in lateral cuts having a depth of an eighth of an inch and are best made with a rat tail file.

Now you can string your bow and test its curve.

Of course, you must have a string, and usually that employed in these early tests is very strong and roughly made of nearly ninety strands of Barbour's linen, No. 12. Directions for making strings will be given later on.

It is difficult to brace a new heavy bow and one will require assistance. In the absence of help he can place it in the vise, one of those revolving on a pivot, and having the string properly adjusted on the lower limb, pull on the upper end in such a way that the other presses against the wall or a stationary brace, thus bending the bow while you slip the expectant loop over the open nock. Or you can have an assistant pull on the upper nock, while you brace the bow yourself.

In ancient times, at this stage, the bow was tillered, or tested for its curve, or, as Sir Roger Ascham says, "brought round compass," which means to make it bend in a perfect arc when full drawn.

The tiller is a piece of board three feet long, two inches wide, and one inch thick, having a V-shaped notch at the lower end to fit on the handle and small notches on its side two inches apart, for a distance of twenty-eight inches. These are to hold the string.

Lay the braced bow on the floor, place the end of the tiller on the handle while you steady the tiller upright. Then put your foot on the bow next the tiller and draw the string up until it slips in the first notch, say twelve inches from the handle. If the curve of the bow is fairly symmetrical, draw the string a few inches more. If again it describes a perfect arc raise the string still farther. A perfect arc for a bow should be a trifle flat at the center. If, on the other hand, one limb or a part of it does not bend as it should, this must be reduced carefully by shaving it for a space of several inches over the spot and the bow tested again.

Proceeding very cautiously, at the same time not keeping the bow full drawn more than a second or two at a time, you ultimately get the two limbs so that they bend nearly the same and the general distribution of the curve is equal throughout.

As a matter of fact, a great deal of experience is needed here. By marking a correct form on the floor with chalk, a novice may fit his bow to this outline.

The perfect weapon is a trifle stiff at the center and the lower limb a shade stronger than the upper.

The real shooting center, the place where the arrow passes, is actually one and one-quarter inches above the geographic center, and the hand consequently is below this point. Your finished hand grip, being four inches long, will be one and a quarter inches above the center and two and three-quarters below the center. This makes the lower limb comparatively shorter, so it must be relatively stronger. Your bow, therefore, when full drawn should be symmetrical, but when simply braced, the bend of the upper limb is perceptibly greater than the stronger lower limb.

You will find the bow we have made will pull over eighty pounds, even after it is thoroughly broken to the string. It is necessary, therefore, to reduce it further. This is done with a spoke shave, a very small hand plane or a file. Ultimately I use a pocket knife as a scraper, and sandpaper and steelwool to finish it.

Your effort must be to get every part of the wood to do its work, for every inch is under utmost strain, and one part doing more than the rest must ultimately break down, sustain a compression fracture, or, as an archer would say, "chrysal or fret."

"A bow full drawn is seven-eighths broken," said old Thomas Waring, the English bowmaker, and he was right. Draw your bow three inches more than the standard cloth yard of twenty-eight inches and you break it. It is more accurate to say that a full drawn bow is nine-tenths broken.

It is also essential that the bow be stiff in the handle so that it will be rigid in shooting and not jar or kick, which one weak at this point invariably does.

A bow should be light at the tips, say the last eight inches, which is accomplished by rounding the back slightly and reducing the width at this point. This gives an active recoil, or as it is described, "whip ended." This can be overdone, especially in hunting-bows, where a little more solidity and safety are preferable to a brilliant cast.

And so you must work and test your bow, and shoot it, and draw it up before a full length mirror and observe its outline, and get your friends to draw it up and pass judgment on it. In fact, while the actual work of making a bow takes about eight hours, it requires months to get one adjusted so that it is good. A bow, like a violin, is a work of art. The best in it can only be brought out by infinite care. Like a violin, it is all curved contours, there is not a straight line in it. Many of my bows have been built over completely three or four times. Old Horrible first pulled eighty-five pounds. It was reduced, shortened, whip ended, and worked over again and again so to tune the wood that all parts acted in harmony. Every good bow is a work of love.

Your bow is now ready to shoot, but let us weigh it first. Brace it and put it horizontally in the vise with the string facing you. Take a spring scale registering at least eighty pounds and catch the hook under the string. Draw it until the yardstick registers twenty-eight inches from the string to the back of the bow. Now read the scale; that is its weight.

As a matter of convenience I have devised a stick that facilitates the weighing. I take a dowel and attach to one end by glue and binding a bent piece of iron so fashioned that the extremity serves as a hook to draw the string and the bent portion permits the attachment of the scale. The dowel is marked off in inches so that one can test different lengths of draw. With the bow in the bench vise, this measure hooked on the string and resting on the bow at the arrow plate, the scale is hooked in place, the dowel drawn down to the standard length and the registered weight read off on the scale.

If you still find that your bow is too strong for you, it must be further reduced. Begin all over again with the spoke shave and the file, trying to correct any inequalities that may have existed before and reducing it to what ultimately will be sixty-five pounds. Put on the string and weigh it again and again until you get the weight you want. If you have reduced it too much, cut it down two or four inches; it will be stronger and shoot better.

All yew bows tend to lose in strength after much use, and your new one should pull five pounds more than the required weight. If a bow is put away in a dry, warm place for several years it nearly always increases in strength. In our experience one in constant use lasts from three to five years. The longer the bow, the longer its life. Some, of course, break or come to grief after a short period, others live to honorable old age. Yew bows are in existence today that were made many thousands of years ago, but, of course, they would break if shot. Many bows over one hundred years old are still in use occasionally. I have estimated that the average life of a good bow should exceed one hundred thousand shots, after which time it begins to fret and show other signs of weakness.

Keeping in mind the idea of making your weapon as beautiful, as symmetrical and resilient as possible, free from dead or overstrained areas, work it down with utmost solicitude until it approaches your ideal. Smooth it with sandpaper; finish it with steelwool.

Now comes the process of putting on the nocks. A bow shoots well without them, but is safer with them.

From time immemorial, horn tips have been put on the ends of the limbs to hold the string. We have used rawhide, hardwood, aluminum, bone, elk horn, deer horn, buffalo horn, paper fiber or composition, and cow's horn. The last seems best of all. From your butcher secure a number of horns. With a saw cut off three or four inches of the tip. Place one in a vise and drill a conical hole in it an inch and a quarter deep and half an inch wide. This can be done by using a half-inch drill which has been ground on a carborundum stone to a conical point the proper length. In this hole set a stout piece of wood with glue. This permits you to hold the horn in the vise while you work it.

After the glue has set, take a coarse file and shape the horn nock to the classical shape, which is hard to describe but easy to illustrate. It must have diagonal grooves to hold the string. The nock for the upper limb has also a hole at its extremity to receive the buckskin thong which keeps the upper loop of the string from slipping too far down the bow when unbraced.

The nocks for hunting bows should be short and stout, not over one and a half inches long, for they get a lot of hard usage in their travels. They should also be broader and thicker than those used on target bows.

Two nocks having been roughly finished, they are loosened from their wooden handles by being soaked in boiling water, and are ready for use. Cut the ends of the bow to fit the nocks in such a way that they tip slightly backward when in place, but do not attach them yet.

At this point we back the bow with rawhide. Ordinarily a yew bow properly protected by sapwood requires no backing; but having had many bows break in our hands, we at last took the advice of Ishi and backed them. Since then no bow legitimately used has broken.

The rawhide utilized for this purpose is known to tanners as clarified calfskin. Its principal use is in the manufacture of artificial limbs, drum heads and parchment. Its thickness is not much more than that of writing paper.

Having secured two pieces about three feet in length and two inches wide, soak them in warm water for an hour.

While this is being done, slightly roughen the back of your bow with a file. Place it in the vise and size the back with thin, hot carpenter's glue. When the hide is soft, lay the pieces smooth side down on a board and wipe off the excess water. Quickly size them with hot glue, remove the excess with your finger, turn the pieces over and apply them to the bow. Overlap them at the hand grip for a distance of two or three inches. Smooth them out toward the tips by stroking and expressing all air bubbles and excess glue. Wrap the handle roughly with string to keep the strips from slipping; also bind the tips for a short distance to secure them in place. Remove the bow from the vise and bandage it carefully from tip to tip with a gauze surgical bandage. Set it aside to dry over night. When dry, remove the bandage and string binding, cut off the overlapping edges of the hide and scrape it smooth. Having got it to the required finish, size the exterior again with very thin glue, and it is ready for the final stage.

The tips of the bow having been cut to a conical point and the nocks fitted prior to the backing process the horn nocks are now set on with glue; the ordinary liquid variety will do.

Glue a thin strip of wood on the back of the bow to round out the handle. This should be about one-eighth of an inch thick, one inch wide and three inches long and rounded at the edges.

Bind the center of your bow with heavy fish line to make the handgrip, carefully overlapping the start and finish. A little liquid glue or shellac can be placed on the wood to fix the serving. Some prefer leather or pigskin for a handgrip, but a cord binding keeps the hand from sweating and has an honest feel.

The handle occupies a space of four inches with one and a quarter inches above the center and two and three-quarters below it. Finish off the edges of the cord binding with a band of thin leather half an inch wide. This should be soaked in water, beveled at the edge, sized with glue, put around the bow, and overlapped at the back. I also glue a small piece of leather on the left-hand side of the bow above the handle to prevent the arrow chafing the wood at this spot. This is called the arrow plate and usually is made of mother-of-pearl or bone; leather is better. These finishing pieces are wrapped temporarily with string until they dry.

The bow is then given a final treatment with scraper and steelwool and is ready for the varnish.

The best protection for bows seems to be spar varnish. This keeps out moisture. It has two disadvantages, however; it cracks after much bending, and it is too shiny. The glint or flash of a hunting bow will frighten game. I have often seen rabbits or deer stand until the bow goes off, then jump in time to escape the arrow. At first we believed they saw the arrow; later we found that they saw the flash. Bows really should be painted a dull green or drab color. But we love to see the natural grain of the wood.

The finish I prefer is first of all to give a coat of shellac to the backing, leather trimmings and cord handle. After it is dry, give the wood a good soaking with boiled linseed oil. Using the same oiled cloth place in its center a small wad of cotton saturated with an alcoholic solution of shellac. Rub this quickly over the bow. By repeated oiling and shellacking one produces a French polish that is very durable and elastic.

Permit this to dry and after several days rub the whole weapon with floor wax, giving a final polish with a woolen cloth.

When on a hunt one should carry a small quantity of linseed oil and anoint his bow every day or so with it. Personally I add one part of light cedar oil to two parts of linseed. The fragrance of the former adds to the pleasure of using the latter.

When not in use hang your bow on a peg or nail slipped beneath the upper loop of the string; do not stand it in a corner, this tends to bend the lower limb. Keep it in a warm, dry room; preserve it from bruises and scratches. Wax it and the string often. Care for it as you would a friend; it is your companion in arms.

SUBSTITUTES FOR YEW

Where it is impossible to obtain yew, the amateur bowyer has a large variety of substitutes. Probably the easiest to obtain is hickory, although it is a poor alternative. I believe the pig-nut or smooth bark is the best variety. One should endeavor to get a piece of second growth, white sapwood, and split it so as to get straight grain.

This can be worked on the same general dimensions as yew, but the resulting bow will be found slow and heavy in cast and to have an incurable tendency to follow the string. It will need no rawhide back and will never break.

Osage orange, mulberry, locust, black walnut with the sap wood, red cedar, juniper, tan oak, apple wood, ash, eucalyptus, lancewood, washaba, palma brava, elm, birch, and bamboo are among the many woods from which bows have been made.

With the exception of lancewood, lemon wood, or osage orange, which are hard to get, the next best wood to yew is red Tennessee cedar backed with hickory.

Go to a lumber yard and select a plank of cedar having the fewest knots and the straightest grain. Saw or split a piece out of it six feet long, two inches wide, and about an inch thick. Plane it straight and roughen its two-inch surface with a file. Obtain a strip of white straight-grained hickory six feet long, two inches wide, and a quarter inch thick.

Roughen one surface, spread these two rough surfaces with a good liquid glue and place them together. With a series of clamps compress them tightly. In the absence of clamps, a pile of bricks or weights may be used. After several days it will be dry enough to work.

From this point on it may be treated the same as yew. The hickory backing takes the place of the sap wood.

Cedar has a soft, lively cast and the hickory backing makes it almost unbreakable.

This bow should be bound with linen or silk every few inches like a fishing rod. Several coats of varnish will keep the glue from being affected by moisture or rain.

Since both woods are usually obtainable at any lumber yard, there should be no difficulty in the matter save the mechanical factors involved. These only add zest to the problem. A true archer must be a craftsman.

MAKING A BOWSTRING

A bow without a string is dead; therefore, we must set to work to make one.

Sinew, catgut, and rawhide strings were used by the early archers, but have been abandoned by the more modern. Animal tissue stretches when it is put under strain or subjected to heat and moisture. Silk makes a good string, but it is short-lived and is not so strong as linen.

A comparative test of various strings was made to determine which material is the strongest for bows. Number 3 surgical catgut is apparently a D string on the violin. Taking this as a standard diameter, a series of waxed strings of various substances were made and tested on a spring scale for their breaking point. The results are as follows:

Horsehair breaks at 15 pounds.
Cotton breaks at 18 pounds.
Catgut breaks at 20 pounds.
Silk breaks at 22 pounds.
Irish linen breaks at 28 pounds.
Chinese grass fiber breaks at 32 pounds.

This latter, with similar unusual fibers, is not on the market in the form of thread, so is of no practical use to us.

We use Irish linen or shoemakers' thread. It is Barbour's Number 12. Each thread will stand a strain of six pounds; therefore, a bowstring of fifty strands will suspend a weight of 300 pounds.

A target bow may have a proportionately lighter string than a hunting bow because here a quick cast is desired; but in hunting, security is necessary. We therefore allow one strand of linen for every pound of the bow.

This is the method of manufacturing a bowstring as devised by the late Mr. Maxson and described in *American Archery*. Some few alterations have been introduced to simplify the technique.

It is advisable to take the threads in your hands as you follow the directions.

If you propose making a string for a sixty-five-pound bow, it should have about sixty threads in it, and these are divided into three strands of twenty threads each. Start making the first of these strands by measuring off on the bow a length eight inches beyond each end—that is, sixteen inches longer than your bow. Double your thread back, drawing it through your hand until you reach the beginning. Now repeat the process of laying one thread with another, back and forth, until twenty are in the strand. But these must be so arranged that each is about half an inch shorter than the preceding, thus making the end of the strand tapered.

When twenty are thus stroked into one cord, they are heavily waxed by drawing the strand through the hand and wax, from center to the ends, each way. Now roll the greater part of this strand about your fingers and make a little coil which you compress, but allow about twenty-four inches to remain free and uncoiled. Thus abbreviated it is easier to handle in the subsequent process of twisting it into a cord.

Make two other strands exactly like this, roll them into a compressed coil and lay them aside. Now to form the loop or eye it is necessary to thicken the string at this point with an additional splice. So lay out another strand of twenty threads six feet long. Cut this into six pieces, each twelve inches in length. Take one of these and so pull the ends of the threads that they are made of uneven length, or that the ends become tapered. Wax this splice thoroughly; do this to each one in turn.

Now pick up one of your original strands and apply to its tapered end and lying along the last foot of its length one of the above described splices. Wax the two together. So treat the two other strands.

Grasp the three cords together in your left hand at a point nine inches from the end. With the right hand pick up one strand near this point and twist it between the thumb and finger, away from you, rolling it tight, at the same time pulling it toward you. Seize another strand, twist it from you and pull it toward you. Continue this process with each in succession, and you will find that you are making a rope. By the time the rope is three inches in length, it is long enough to fold on itself and constitute a loop. Proceed to double it back so that the loose ends of the strands are mated and waxed into cohesion with the three main strands of the string. Arrange them nicely so that they interlace properly and are evenly applied.

Now while being seated, slip the upper limb of your bow under your right knee and over the left, and drop the new formed loop of your string over the horn nock. Begin again the process of twisting each strand away from you while you pull it toward you. Continue the motion until you have run down the string a distance of eight inches. During the process you will see the wisdom of having rolled the excess string up into little skeins to keep them from being tangled. Thus the upper eye is formed. At this stage unwind your skeins and stretch the string down the bow, untwisting and drawing straight the three strands.

Seize them now three inches below the lower nock of your bow. At this point apply the short splices for the lower loop. They should be so laid on that three inches extends up the string from this point and the rest lies along the tapered extremity. Wax them tight. Hold the three long strands together while you give them final equalizing traction. Start here and twist your second loop, drawing each strand toward you as you twist it away from you until a rope of three inches is formed again. This you double back on itself, mate its tapered extremities with the three long strands of the string and wax them together.

Slip the upper loop down your bow and nock the lower loop on the lower horn. Swing your right knee over the bow below the string and set the loop on this horn while you work. Give the string plenty of slack.

Start again the twisting and pulling operation, keeping the strands from tangles while you form the lower splice of the string. When it is eight inches long, take off the loop and unroll the twist in the main body of the string. Replace the loop and brace your bow. This will take the kinks from the cord. Wax it thoroughly and, removing the lower loop, twist the entire bowstring in the direction of the previous maneuver until it is shortened to the proper length to fit the bow. Nock the string again and, taking a thick piece of paper, fold it into a little pad and rub the bowstring vigorously until it assumes a round, well-waxed condition.

If the loops are properly placed, the final twisting should make one complete rotation of the string in a distance of one or two inches. A closer twist tends to cut itself.

If, by mistake, the string is too short or too long, and adjusting the twist does not correct it, then you must undo the last loop to overcome the error. The fork of these loops is often bound with waxed carpet thread to reduce their size and strengthen them. The whole structure at this point may be served with the same thread to protect it from becoming chafed and worn.

The center of the string and the nocking point for the arrow must now be served with waxed silk, linen, or cotton thread to protect it from becoming worn.

Ordinarily we take a piece of red carpet thread or shoe button thread, about two yards in length, wax it thoroughly and double it. Start with the doubled end, threading the free end through it around the string, and wind it over, from right to left. The point of starting this serving is two and one-half inches above the center of the bowstring.

When you come to the nocking point, or that at which an arrow stands perpendicular to the string while crossing the bow at the top of the handle, make a series of overlapping threads or clove hitches. This will form a little lump or knot on the string at this point. Continue serving for half an inch and repeat this maneuver; again continue the serving down the string for a distance of four or five inches, finishing with a fixed lashing by drawing the thread under the last two or three wraps.

A nocking point of this character has two advantages: the first is that you can feel it readily while nocking an arrow in the dark or while keeping your eye on the game, and the other point is that the knots prevent the arrow being dislodged while walking through the brush.

We have found that by heating our beeswax and adding about one-quarter rosin, it makes it more adhesive.

In hot or wet weather it is of some advantage to rub the string with an alcoholic solution of shellac. Compounds containing glue or any hard drying substance seem to cause the strings to break more readily. Paraffin, talcum powder, or a bit of tallow candle rubbed on the serving and nocking point is useful in making a clean release of the string.

So far as dampness and rain go, these never interfere with the action of the string. A well-greased bow will stand considerable water, though arrows suffer considerably.

Wax your string every few days if in use; you should always carry an extra one with you.

Strings break most commonly at the nocking point beneath the serving. Here they sustain the greatest strain and are subject to most bending. An inspection at this point frequently should be done. An impending break is indicated by an uneven contour of the strands beneath the serving. Discard it before it actually breaks.

By putting a spring scale between one of the bow nocks and the end of the string, the unexpected phenomenon is demonstrated that there is greater tension on a string when the bow is braced but not drawn up. A fifty-six pound bow registers a sixty-four pound tension on the string. As the arrow is drawn up the tension decreases gradually until twenty-six inches are drawn, when it registers sixty-four pounds again.

At the moment of recoil, when the bow springs back into position, this strain must rise tremendously, for if the arrow be not in place the string frequently will be broken.

The tension on the string at the center or nocking point during the process of drawing a bow—that is, the accumulated weight—rises quite differently in different bows. The arrow being nocked on the string, it is ordinarily already six inches drawn across the bow. Now in the same fifty-six pound bow for every inch of draw past this, the weight rises between two and three pounds. As the arrow nears full draw, the weight increases to such a degree that the last few inches will register five or six pounds to the inch, depending on many variable factors in the bow.

The gradient thus formed dictates the character of a bow to a great extent. One that pulls softly at first and in the last part of the draw is very stiff, will require more careful shooting to get the exact length of flight than one whose tension is evenly distributed.

Reflexed bows are harder on strings than those that follow the string. A breaking cord may fracture your bow. I saw Wallace Bryant lose a beautiful specimen this way. One of Aldred's most perfect make, dark Spanish yew and more than fifty years old, flew to splinters just because a treacherous string parted in the center. Sturdy hunting bows are not so liable to this catastrophe, but be sure you are not caught out in a game country with a broken string and no second. You will see endless opportunities to shoot. Wax is to an archer what tar is to a sailor; use it often, and always have two strings to your bow.

VI

HOW TO MAKE AN ARROW

Fletching is a very old art and, necessarily, must have many empirical methods and principles involved. There are innumerable types of arrows, and an equal number of ways of making them. For an excellent description of a good way to make target arrows, the reader is referred to that chapter by Jackson in the book *American Archery*.

Having learned several aboriginal methods of fletching and studied all the available literature on the subject, we have adopted the following maneuvers to turn out standard hunting arrows: The first requisite is the shaft. Having tested birch, maple, hickory, oak, ash, poplar, alder, red cedar, mahogany, palma brava, Philippine nara, Douglas fir, red pine, white pine, spruce, Port Orford cedar, yew, willow, hazel, eucalyptus, redwood, elderberry, and bamboo, we have adopted birch as the most rigid, toughest and suitable in weight for hunting arrows. Douglas fir and Norway pine are best for target shafts; bamboo for flight arrows.

The commercial dowel, frequently called a maple dowel, is made of white birch and is exactly suited to our purpose. It may be obtained in quantities from dealers in hardwoods, or from sash and door mills. If possible, you should select these dowels yourself, to see that they are straight, free from cross-grain, and of a rigid quality. For hunting bows drawing over sixty pounds, the dowels should be three-eighths of an inch in diameter; for lighter bows five-sixteenths dowels should be used. They come in three-foot lengths and bundles of two hundred and fifty. It is a good plan to buy a bundle at a time and keep them in the attic to dry and season.

Where dowels are not obtainable, you can have a hickory or birch plank sawed up or split into sticks half an inch in diameter, and plane these to the required size, or turn them on a lathe, or run them through a dowel-cutting machine.

Take a dozen dowels from your stock and cut them to a length of twenty-eight and one-quarter inches, or an inch less or more according to the length of your arms. In doing this you should try to remove the worst end, keeping that portion with the straightest grain for the head of your shaft.

Having cut them to length, take a hand plane and shave the last six inches of the rear end or shaftment so that the diameter is reduced to a trifle more than five-sixteenths of an inch at the extremity.

Now comes the process of straightening your shafts. By squinting down the length of the dowel you can observe the crooked portions. If these are very bad, they should be heated gently over a gas flame and then bent into proper line over the base of the thumb or palm. A pair of gloves will protect the hand from burning. If the deviation be slight, then mere manual pressure is often sufficient. During this process the future arrow should be tested for strength. If it cannot stand considerable bending it deserves to break. If it is limber, discard it.

Nocking the shaft comes next. Hunting arrows require no horn, bone, aluminum, or fiber nock. Simply place the smaller end of the shaft in a vise and cut the end across the grain with three hack saws bound together, your cut being about an eighth of an inch wide by three-eighths deep; finish it carefully with a file. Thus nock them all and sandpaper them smooth throughout, rounding the nocked end gracefully. To facilitate this process I place one end in a motor-driven chuck and hold the rapidly revolving shaft in a piece of sandpaper in my hand. When finished the diameter should be a trifle under three-eighths of an inch at the center and about five-sixteenths at the nock.

Mark them now, where the feathers and binding should go. At a point one inch from the base of the nock make a circular line, this is for the rear binding; five inches above this make another, this is for the feather; one inch above this make another, this is for the front binding; and an inch above this make another, this is for the painted ribbon.

Feathers come next, but really they should have come long ago. The best are turkey feathers, so we won't talk about any others. The time to get them is at Thanksgiving and Christmas. Then you should get on good terms with your butcher and have him save you a boxful of turkey wings. These you chop with a hatchet on a block, saving only the six or seven long pinions. Put them away with moth balls until you need them. Of course, if you cannot get turkey feathers when you want them, goose, chicken, duck, or plumes from a feather duster may be employed. Your milliner can tell you where to purchase goose feathers, but these are expensive.

Cutting arrow feathers is a pleasant occupation around the fire in the winter evenings, and the real archer has the happiness of making his tackle while his mind dwells upon the coming spring shooting. As he makes his shaft he wonders what fate will befall it. Will it speed away in a futile shot, or last the grilling of a hundred practice flights, or will it be that fortunate arrow which flies swift and true and brings down the bounding deer? How often have I picked up a shaft and marked it, saying, "With this I'll kill a bear." And with some I've done it, too!

So your feathers should be cut in quantity. This is the way you cut them: Select a good clean one, steady it between your palms while with your fingers you separate the bristles at the tip. Pull them apart, thus splitting the rib down the center. If by chance it should not split evenly, take your sharpened penknife and cut it straight.

Have ready a little spring clip, such as is used to hold your cravat or magazine in a book store. One end of this is bent about a safety-pin so that it can be fastened to your trousers at the knee. Now you have a sort of knee vise to hold your feather while trimming it. Place the butt of the rib in the jaws of the clip and shave it down to the thickness of a thirty-second of an inch. Make this even and level so that the feather stands perpendicular to it. With a pair of long scissors cut off the lateral excess of rib on the concave side of the feather. This permits it to straighten out.

At the same stage cut the feather roughly to shape; that is, five inches long, half an inch at the anterior end, an inch wide posteriorly, and having an inch of stem projecting at each extremity.

For this work you must keep your pocket-knife very sharp. With practice you should cut a feather in two or three minutes.

Donnan Smith, a worthy archer and a good fletcher, has devised a spring clamp which holds the feather while being cut. It is composed of a strong binder clip to which are soldered two thin metal jaws the size and shape of a properly cut feather. Having stripped his feather, he clamps it rib uppermost between the jaws and trims the rib with a knife, or on a fast-revolving emery stone, or sandpaper disc. This accomplished, he turns the feather around in the clamp and cuts the bristles to the exact shape of the metal jaws with a pair of scissors. It is an admirable method.

Some fletchers cut their feathers on a board by eye with only a knife. James Duff, the well-known American maker of tackle, learned this in the shop of Peter Muir, the famous Scotch fletcher.

If you wish to dye your feathers it may be done by obtaining the aniline dye used on wool. Adding about 10 per cent of vinegar to the aqueous solution of the stain, heat it to such a temperature that you can just stand your finger in it. Soak your feathers in this hot solution, stir them for several minutes, then lay them out on a piece of newspaper to dry in the sun. Red, orange, and yellow are used for this purpose; the former helps one to find a lost arrow, but all colors tend to run if wet, and stain the clothing.

Having prepared a sufficient quantity of feathers, you are ready to fledge your shaft. Select three of a similar color, strength, and from the same wing of the bird. With a stick, run a little liquid glue along the rib of each and lay it aside. Along the axis of your arrow run three parallel lines of glue down the shaftment. The first of these is for the cock feather and should be on a line perpendicular to the nock. The other two are equidistant from this. A novice should mark these lines with a pencil at first.

Now comes a difficult task, that of putting on the feathers. Many ways and means have been devised, and in target arrows nothing is better than just sticking them on by hand. Some have used clamps, some use pins, some lash the feathers on at the extremities with thread, and then glue beneath them. We take the oldest of all methods, which is shown in the specimens of old Saxon arrows rescued from the Nylander boat in Holland, also depicted in many old English paintings—that of binding the feathers with a piece of thread running spirally up the shaft between the bristles.

Starting at a point six inches from the nock, set your thick end of the rib in position on the lines of glue. Hold the shaft under your left arm while with the left thumb, forefinger, and middle finger steady the feathers as they are respectively put in place. With one end of a piece of cotton basting thread in your teeth and the spool in your right hand, start binding the ribs down to the arrow shaft. After a few turns proceed up the shaftment, adjusting the feathers in position as you rotate the arrow. Let your basting thread slip between the bristles of the feather about half an inch apart. When you come to the rear end, finish up with several overlapping turns and a half-hitch. Line up your feathers so that they run straight down the shaftment and are equidistant. Of one thing be very sure—see that your feather runs a trifle toward the concave side, looking from the rear, and that the rear end deviates quite perceptibly toward this direction. This insures proper steering qualities to your arrow. Set it aside and let it dry.

When all are dry, remove the basting thread and trim the ribs to the pencil marks, leaving them about three-quarters of an inch long. Bevel their ends to a slender taper.

The next process is that of binding the feathers in position. The material which we use for this purpose is known as ribonzine, a thin silk ribbon used to bind candy boxes. In the absence of this, floss silk may be employed. Cut it into pieces about a foot long. Put a little liquid glue on the space reserved for binding and, while revolving the shaft under your arm, apply the ribbon in lapping spirals over the feather ribs. Cover them completely and have the binding smooth and well sized in glue. The ribbon near the nock serves to protect the wood at this point from splitting. When dry, clean your shaft from ragged excess of glue with knife and sandpaper, and finish up by running a little diluted glue with a small brush along the side of the feather ribs to make them doubly secure.

Now comes the painting.

We paint arrows not so much for gayness, as to preserve them against moisture, to aid in finding them when lost, and to distinguish one man's shaft from another's.

Chinese vermilion and bright orange are colors which are most discernible in the grass and undergrowth. With a narrow brush, paint between your feathers, running up slightly on to the rib, covering the glue. If your silk ribbon binding is a bright color—mine is green—you can leave it untouched. We often paint the nock a distinguishing color to indicate the type of head at the other end, so that in drawing the shaft from the quiver we can know beforehand what sort it will be. The livery should be painted in several different rings. My own colors are red, green, and white.

One or two coats are applied according to the fancy of the archer. The line between the various pigments should be striped with a thin black ring.

Unless you use a lathe to hold your arrows in the painting process, you can employ two wooden blocks or rests, one having a shallow countersunk hole on its lateral face to hold the nock while rotating, the other having a groove on its upper surface. Clamp these on a bench, or on the opposite arms of your easy chair before the fire, and you can turn your shafts slowly by hand while you steady your brush and apply the paint in even rings.

At this stage I have added a device which seems to be helpful in nocking arrows in the dark, or while keeping one's eye on the game. Having put a drop of glue on the ribbon immediately above the nock and behind the cock feather, I affix a little white glass bead. One can feel this with his thumb as he nocks his arrow, when in conjunction with knots on his string, he can perform this maneuver entirely by touch.

The paint having dried, varnish or shellac your arrow its entire length, avoiding, of course, any contact with the feathers. In due time sandpaper the shaft and repeat the varnishing. Rub this down with steelwool and give it a finishing touch with floor wax.

Here we are ready for the arrow-heads.

We use three types of points. The first is a blunt head made by binding the end of the shaft with thin tinned iron wire for half an inch and running on solder, then drilling a hole in the end of the shaft and inserting an inch round-headed screw. In place of soldered wire, one can use an empty 38-caliber cartridge, either cutting off the base or drilling out the priming aperture to admit the screw. This type of arrow we use for rough practice, shooting tin cans, trees, boxes, and other impedimenta. It makes a good shaft for birds, rabbits, and small game.

A second type of head we use is made of soft steel about a sixteenth of an inch thick. We cut it with a hack saw into a blunt, barbed, lanceolate shape having a blade about an inch long and half an inch wide, also a tang about the same length and three-eighths of an inch wide.

This we set into a slot sawed in the arrow in the same plane as the nock, and bind the shaft with tinned wire, number 30, soldered together. The end of the shaft has a gradual bevel where it meets the lateral face of the head.

This is a sturdy little point and will stand much abuse. We use it for shooting birds, squirrels, and small vermin.

But the point that we prefer to shoot is the old English broad-head. Starting from small dimensions, we have gradually increased its size, weight and strength and cutting qualities till now we shoot a head whose blade is three inches long, an inch and a quarter wide, a trifle less than a thirty-second thick. It has a haft or tubular shank an inch long. Its weight is half an ounce. The blades are made of spring steel. After annealing the steel we score it diagonally with a hack saw, when it may be broken in triangular pieces in a vise. With a cold chisel, an angular cut is made in the base to form the barbs. With a file and carborundum stone, they are edged and shaped into blades as sharp as knives. Soft, cold drawn steel will serve quite as well as spring steel for these blades, but it does not hold its edge. It may be purchased at hardware supply depots in the form of strips an inch and a half wide, by one-thirty-second thick, and is much easier to work than the tempered variety.

Then taking three-eighths number .22 gauge steel or brass tubing, we smash it to a short bevel on the anvil, file off the corners and cut it to a length of an inch and three-quarters. This makes the haft or socket. Fixing a blade, barbs uppermost in the vise, this tubing is driven lightly into position, the filed edges of the beveled end permitting the blade to be held between the sides of the tubing. A small hole is drilled through the tubing and blade, and a soft iron wire rivet is inserted. The blade is held over a gas flame while the joint between it and the tubing is filled with soft soldering compound and ribbon solder.

The heated head is plunged into water and later finished with file and emery cloth. The whole process of making a steel broad-head requires about twenty minutes. Every archer should manufacture his own. Then he will treat them with more respect. Very few artisans can make them, and if they can, their price is exorbitant.

Be sure that your heads are straight and true. To set them on your shaft, cut the wood to fit, then heat a bit of ferrule cement and set them on in the same plane as the nock. In the absence of ferrule cement, which can be had at all sporting goods stores, one can use chewing gum, or better yet, a mixture of caoutchouc pitch and scale shellac heated together in equal parts. Heat your fixative as you would sealing wax, over a candle, also heat the arrow and the metal head. Put on with these adhesives, it seldom pulls off. In the wilds we often fix the head with pine resin. Glue can be used, but it is not so good.

Having brought your arrows to this stage, the next act is to trim the feathers. First run them gently through the hand and smooth out their veins; then with long-bladed scissors cut them so that the anterior end is three-eighths of an inch high, while the posterior extremity is one inch. I also cut the rear tip of the feather diagonally across, removing about half an inch to prevent it getting in the way of the fingers when on the string.

Mr. Arthur Young cuts his feathers in a long parabola with a die made of a knife blade bent into shape. These things are largely a matter of taste.

Look your arrows over; see that they are straight and that the feathers are in good shape, then shoot them to observe their flight. Number them above the ribbon so that you can keep record of their performances. The weight of such an arrow is one and one-half ounces.

The small blunt, barb-headed arrows we often paint red their entire length. Because they are meant for use in the brush, they are more readily lost; the bright color saves many a shaft.

To make a hunting arrow requires about an hour, and one should be willing to look for one almost this time when it is lost. Finding arrows is an acquired art. Don't forget the advice of Bassanio: "In my school days when I had lost one shaft, I shot his fellow of the self-same flight, the self-same way, with more advised watch to find the other forth; and by adventuring both, I oft found both."

If, indeed, the shaft cannot be found, then give it up with good grace, remembering that after all it is pleasant work to make one. Dedicate it to the cause of archery with the hope that in future days some one may pick it up and, pricking his finger on the barb, become inoculated with the romance of archery.

When an arrow lodges in a root or tree, we work the head back and forth very carefully to withdraw it. A little pair of pliers comes in very handy here. If it is buried deeply we cut the wood away from it with a hunting knife. Blunt arrows, called bird bolts by Shakespeare, are best to shoot up in the branches of trees at winged and climbing game.

In our quivers we usually carry several light shafts we call eagle arrows, because they are designed principally for shooting at this bird.

Once while hunting deer, and observing a doe and fawn drinking at a pool, we saw a magnificent golden eagle swoop down, catch the startled fawn and lift it from the ground. Mr. Compton and I, having such arrows in our quivers, let fly at the struggling bird of prey. We came so close that the eagle loosened the grip of his talons and the fawn dropped to earth and sped off with its mother, safe for the time being.

Often we have shot at hawks and eagles high up in the air, where to reach them we needed a very light arrow, and they have had many close calls. For these we use a five-sixteenths dowel, feather it with short, low cut parabolic feathers and put a small barbed head on it about an inch in length. Such an arrow we paint dark green, blue, or black, so that the bird cannot discern its flight.

It is great sport to shoot at some lazy old buzzard as he comes within range. He can see the ordinary arrow, and if you shoot close, he dodges, swoops downward, flops sidewise, twists his head round and round, and speeds up to leave the country. He presents the comic picture of a complacent old gentleman suddenly disturbed in his monotonous existence and frightened into a most unbecoming loss of dignity.

Eagle arrows can be used for lofty flights, to span great canyons, to rout the chattering bluejay from the topmost limb of a pine, and sooner or later we shall pierce an eagle on the wing.

We make another kind of shaft that we call a "floo-floo." In Thompson's *Witchery of Archery* he describes an arrow that his Indian companion used, which gave forth such a fluttering whistle when in flight that they called it by this euphonious name. This is made by constructing the usual blunt screw-headed shaft and fledging it with wide uncut feathers. It is useful in shooting small game in the brush, because its flight is impeded and, missing the game, it soon loses momentum and stops. It does not bound off into the next county, but can be found near by. As a rule, these are steady, straight fliers for a short distance.

In finishing the nock of an arrow, it should be filed so that it fits the string rather snugly, thus when in place it is not easily disturbed by the ordinary accidents of travel. Still this tightness should be at the entrance of the nock, while the bottom of the nock is made a trifle more roomy with a round file. I file all my nocks to fit a certain two-inch wire nail whose diameter is just that of my bowstring.

After arrows have been shot for a time and their feathers have settled, they should again be trimmed carefully to their final proportions. The heads, if found too broad for perfect flight, should be ground a trifle narrower.

When hunting, one does well to carry in his pocket a small flat file with which to sharpen his broad-heads before shooting them. They should have a serrated, meat-cutting edge. Even carrying arrows in a quiver tends to dull them, because they chafe each other while in motion. From time to time you should rub the shafts and heads with the mixture of cedar and linseed oil, thus keeping them clean and protected from dampness.

On a hunting trip an archer should carry with him in his repair kit, extra feathers, heads, cement, a tube of glue, ribonzine, linen thread, wax, paraffin, sandpaper, emery cloth, pincers, file and small scissors. With these he can salvage many an arrow that otherwise would be too sick to shoot.

Extra arrows are carried in a light wooden box which has little superimposed racks on which they rest and are kept from crushing each other.

As a rule, nothing does an arrow so much good as to shoot it, and nothing so much harm as to have it lie inactive and crowded in the quiver.

The flight of an arrow is symbolic of life itself. It springs from the bow with high aim, flies toward the blue heaven above, and seems to have immortal power. The song of its life is sweet to the ear. The rush of its upward arc is a promise of perpetual progress. With perfect grace it sweeps onward, though less aspiring. Then fluttering imperceptibly, it points downward and with ever-increasing speed, approaches the earth, where, with a deep sigh, it sinks in the soil, quivers with spent energy, and capitulates to the inevitable.

VII

ARCHERY EQUIPMENT

Besides a bow and arrow, the archer needs to have a quiver, a bow case, a waterproof quiver case, an arm guard or bracer, and a shooting glove or leather finger tips. Our quivers are made of untanned deer hide, usually from deer shot with the bow. The hide, having been properly cleaned, stretched, and dried, is cut down the center, each half making a quiver. Marking a quadrilateral outline twenty-four inches on two sides, twelve at the larger end, and nine at the smaller, in such a way that the hair points from the larger to the smaller end; cut this piece and soak it in water until soft, and wash it clean with soap. At the same time cut a circular piece off the tough neck skin, three inches in diameter.

With a furrier's needle having three sharp edges, and heavy waxed thread, or better yet, with catgut, sew up the longer sides of the skin with a simple overcast stitch. Let the hair side be in while sewing. In the smaller end sew the circular bottom. Invert the quiver on a stick; turn back a cuff of hide one inch deep at the top. To do this nicely, the hair should be clipped away at this point. This cuff stiffens the mouth of the quiver and keeps it always open.

Now put your quiver over a wooden form to dry.

I have one like a shoemaker's last, made of two pieces of wood separated by a thin slat which can be removed, permitting easy withdrawal of the quiver after drying. When dry, your quiver will be about twenty-two inches deep, four inches across the top, and slightly conical.

Cut a strip of deer hide eight inches long by one and a half wide, shave it, double the hair side in, and attach it to the seamy side of the quiver by perforating the leather and inserting a lacing of buckskin thongs. Leave the loop of this strap projecting two inches above the top of the quiver. In the bottom of your quiver drop a round piece of felt or carpet to prevent the arrow points coming through the hide.

If you are not so fortunate as to have deer hide, you may use any stiff leather, or even canvas. This latter can be made stiff by painting or varnishing it.

Such a receptacle will hold a dozen broad-heads very comfortably and several more under pressure. It should swing from a belt at the right hip in such a way that in walking it does not touch the leg, while in shooting it is accessible to the right hand or may then be shifted slightly to the front for convenience.

In running we usually grasp the quiver in the right hand, not only to prevent it interfering with locomotion, but to keep the arrows from rattling and falling out. When on the trail of an animal we habitually stuff a twig of leaves, a bunch of ferns or a bit of grass in the mouth of the quiver to damp the soft rustling of the arrows. Sometimes, in going through brush or when running, we carry the quiver on a belt slung over the left shoulder. Here they are out of the way and give the legs full action.

To keep the arrows dry, and to cover them while traveling, we make a sheath for the quiver of waterproof muslin. This is long enough to cover the arrows and has a wire ring a bit larger than the top of the quiver sewn in the cloth some three inches from the upper end. This keeps the feathers from being crushed. The mouth of this cover is closed with a drawstring. On the side adjacent to the strap of the quiver, an aperture is cut to permit this being brought through and fastened to the belt.

The bow itself has a long narrow case made of the same cloth, or canvas, or green baize with a drawstring at the top and a leather tip at the bottom. Where several bows are packed together, each has a woolen bow case and all are carried in a canvas bag, composition carrying cylinder, or in a wooden bow box. In hunting we prefer the canvas bag, but you must carry it yourself, any one else will break your bows.

The bracer, or arm guard, is a cuff of leather worn on the left forearm to prevent the stroke of the bowstring doing damage. Some archers can shoot without this protection, but others, because of their style of shooting or their anatomical formation, need it. It can be made like a butcher's cuff, some six or eight inches long, partially surrounding the forearm and fastened by three little straps or by lacing in the back. Another form is simply a strip of thin sole leather from two to three inches wide by eight long, having little straps and buckles attached to hold it in position on the flexor surface of the wrist and forearm.

The bracer not only keeps the arm from injury, but makes for a clean release of the arrow. Anything such as a coat sleeve touching the bowstring when in action, diverts the arrow in its flight. On the sleeve of your shooting jersey you can sew a piece of leather for an arm guard.

While one may pick up a bow and shoot a few shots without a glove or finger protection, he soon will be compelled to cease because of soreness. Doubtless the ancient yeoman, a horny-handed son of toil, needed no glove. But we know that even in those days a tab of leather was held in the hand to prevent the string from hurting. The glove probably is of more modern use and quite in favor among target archers. We have found it rather hot in hunting, so have resorted to leather finger tips. These are best made of pigskin or cordovan leather, which is horse hide. This should be about a sixteenth of an inch thick and cut to such a form that the tips enclose the finger on the palmar surface up to the second joint and leave an oval opening over the knuckle and upper part of the finger nail. The best way to make them is to mould a piece of paper about each of the first three fingers on the right hand, gathering the paper on the back and crimping it with the thumb nail to show where to cut the pattern. Lay the paper out flat and cut it approximately according to the illustrated form.

Transferring these outlines to the leather, cut three pieces accordingly, soak them in water and sew them. This stitching is best done by previously punching holes along the edges with a fine awl and sewing an overcast stitch of waxed linen thread which, having reached the end, returns backward on its course through the same holes. This makes a criss-cross effect which is strong and pleasing to the eye.

The ends of the finger cots should be sewed closed, protecting the fingers from injury and keeping out dirt. While the leather is still soft and damp, place the tips on the fingers and press them home. At the same time flex them strongly at the joints and try to keep them bent there. Such angulation helps not only in holding the bowstring, but keeps the tip from coming off under pressure. When dry, these leather stalls should be numbered according to the finger to which they belong, coated lightly with thin glue on the inside and waxed on the outer surface. Then they are ready for use.

An archer should have two sets of tips so that, should misfortune befall him and he loses one, he is not altogether undone. When not in use keep them in your pocket or strung on the strap of your bracer. In by-gone days they were sewed to straps which fastened to a wrist belt, thus were more secure from loss, but more cumbersome.

From time to time oil your tips and always keep them from being roughened or scratched. With a small amount of glue in the tip one has only to moisten his fingers in his mouth and the leather stall will stick on firmly. We have also used lead plaster of the pharmacopoeia for the same adhesive purpose.

In the absence of pockets in ancient days, the archer carried his extra equipment in a wallet slung at his waist. Even now it seems a handy thing to have a deerskin wallet six by eight inches, by an inch or more deep. I frequently carry my tips, extra string, wax, file wrapped in a cloth, and a bit of lunch, in such a receptacle.

With his bow, his quiver, a wallet, our modern archer is ready and could step into Sherwood Forest feeling quite at home.

VIII

HOW TO SHOOT

First, brace your bow. To do this properly, grasp it at the handle with your right hand, the upper horn upward and the back toward you. Place the lower horn at the instep of your right foot, and the base of your left palm against the back of the bow, near the top below the loop of the string. Holding your left arm stiff and toward your left side, your right elbow fixed on your hip, pull up on the handle by twisting your body so that the bow is sprung away from you. The string is now relaxed, and the fingers of the left hand push it upward till it slips in the nock.

Don't try to force the string, and don't get your fingers caught beneath it. Do most of the work with the right hand pulling against the rigid left arm.

The proper distance between the bow and the string at the handle is six inches. This is ordinarily measured by setting the fist on the handle and the thumb sticking upright, where it should touch the string. This is the ancient fistmele, an archer's measure, also used in measuring lumber.

Hunting bows should be strung a little less than this because of the prolonged strain on them. Target bows shoot cleaner when higher strung.

Change your bow to your left hand and drop the arm so that the upper end of the bow swings across the body in a horizontal position. Draw an arrow from the quiver with the right hand and carry it across the bow till it rests on the left side at the top of the handle. Place the left forefinger over the shaft and keep it from slipping while you shift your right hand to the arrow-nock, thumb uppermost. Push the arrow forward, at the same time rotating it until the cock feather, or that perpendicular to the nock, is away from the bow. As the feathers pass over the string and the thumb still rests on the nock, slip the fingers beneath the string and fit it in the arrow-nock.

Now turn the bow upright and remove your left forefinger from its position across the shaft. The arrow should rest on the knuckles without lateral support. Now place your fingers in position for shooting. The release used by the old English is the best. This consists in placing three fingers on the string, one above the arrow, two below. The string rests midway between the last joint and the tip of the finger. The thumb should not touch the arrow, but lie curled up in the palm.

The release used by children consists in pinching the arrow between the thumb and forefinger, and is known as the primary loose. This type is not strong enough to draw an arrow half way on a hunting bow.

Stand sidewise to your mark, with the feet eight or ten inches apart, at right angles to the line of shot. Straighten your body, stiffen the back, expand the chest, turn the head fully facing the mark, look at it squarely, and draw your bow across the body, extending the left arm as you draw the right hand toward the chin.

Draw the arrow steadily, in the exact plane of your mark, so that when the full draw is obtained and the arrowhead touches the left hand, the right forefinger touches a spot on the jaw perpendicularly below the right eye and the right elbow is in a continuous line with the arrow. This point on the jaw below the eye is fixed and never varies; no matter how close or how far the shot, the butt of the arrow is always drawn to the jaw, not to the eye, nor to the ear. Thus the eye glances along the entire length of the shaft and keeps it in perfect line. The bow hand may be lowered or raised to obtain the proper elevation and length of flight. The left arm is held rigidly but not absolutely extended and locked at the elbow. A slight degree of flexion here makes for a good clearance of the string and adds resiliency to the shot.

The arrow is released by drawing the right hand further backward at the same time the fingers slip off the string. This must be done so firmly, yet deftly, that no loss of power results, and the releasing hand does not draw the arrow out of line. Two great faults occur at this point: one is to permit the arrow to creep forward just before the release, and the other is to draw the hand away from the face in the act of releasing. Keep your fingers flexed and your hand by your jaw. All the fingers of the right hand must bear their proper share of work. The great tendency is to permit the forefinger to shirk and to put too much work on the ring finger.

If the arrow has a tendency to fall away from the bow, tip the upper limb ten degrees to the right and pull more on the right forefinger, also start the draw with the fingers more acutely flexed, so that as the arrow is pinched between the first and second fingers and as they tend to straighten out under the pressure of the string, the arrow is pressed against the bow, not away from it.

In grasping the bow with the left hand, it should rest comfortably in the palm and loosely at the beginning of the draw. The knuckle at the base of the thumb should be opposite the center of the bow, the hand set straight on the wrist. As you draw, be sure that the arrow comes up in a straight line with your mark, otherwise the bow will be twisted in the grasp and deflect the shot. Then fully drawn, set the grasp of the left hand without disturbing the position of the bow, make the left arm as rigid as an oak limb; fix the muscles of the chest; make yourself inflexible from head to toe. Keep your right elbow up and rivet your gaze upon your mark; release in a direct line backward. Everything must be under the greatest tension, any weakening spoils your flight.

The method of aiming in game shooting consists in fixing binocular vision on the object to be hit, drawing the nock of the arrow beneath the right eye and observing that the head of the arrow is in a direct line with the mark by the indirect vision of the right eye. Both eyes are open, both see the mark, but only the right observes the arrowhead, the left ignores it. Your vision must be so concentrated upon one point that all else fades from view. Just two things exist—your mark and your arrowhead.

At a range of sixty or eighty yards, the head of the arrow seems to touch the mark while aiming. This is called point blank range. At shorter lengths the archer must estimate the distance below the mark on which his arrow seems to rest in order to rise in a parabolic curve and strike the spot. At greater ranges he must estimate a distance above the mark on which he holds his arrow in order to drop it on the object of his shot.

If his shaft flies to the left, it is because he has not drawn the nock beneath his right eye, or he has thrown his head out of line, or the string has hit his shirt sleeve or something has deflected the arrow.

If it falls to the right, it is because he has made a forward, creeping release, or weakened in his bow arm, or in drawing to the center of the jaw instead of the angle beneath the eye.

If the arrow rattles on the bow as it is released, or slaps it hard in passing, it is because it is not drawn up in true line, or because it fits too tightly on the string, or because the release is creeping and weak. Always draw fully up to the barb.

If his arrows drop low and all else is right, it is because he has not kept his tension, or has lowered his bow arm.

After the arrow is released, the archer should hold his posture a second, bow arm rigidly extended, drawing hand to his jaw, right elbow horizontal. This insures that he maintains the proper position during the shot. There should be no jerking, swinging, or casting motions; all must be done evenly and deliberately.

The shaft should fly from the bowstring like a bird, without quaver or flutter. All depends upon a sharp resilient release.

Having observed all the prerequisites of good shooting, nothing so insures a keen, true arrow flight as an effort of supreme tension during the release. The chest is held rigid in a position of moderate inspiration, the back muscles are set and every tendon is drawn into elastic strain; in fact, to be successful, the whole act should be characterized by the utmost vigor.

To get the best instructions for shooting the bow, one should read Sir Roger Ascham in *Toxophilus*, and Horace Ford on *Archery*.

Game shooting differs from target shooting in that with the latter a point of aim is used, and the archer fixes his eyes upon this point which is perpendicular above or below the bull's-eye. The arrowhead is held on the point of aim, and when loosed, flies not along the line of vision, but describes a curve upward, descends and strikes not the point of aim, but the bull's-eye.

The field archer should learn to estimate distances correctly by eye. He should practice pacing measured lengths, so that he can tell how many yards any object may be from him.

In hunting he should make a mental note of this before he shoots. In fact we nearly always call the number of yards before we loose the arrow.

Where a strong cross-wind exists, a certain amount of windage is allowed. But up to sixty yards the lateral deflexion from wind is negligible; past this it may amount to three or four feet.

In clout shooting and target practice, one must take wind into consideration. In hunting we only consider it when approaching game, as a carrier of scent, because our hunting ranges are well under a hundred yards and our heavy hunting shafts tack into the wind with little lateral drift.

No matter how much a man may shoot, he is forever struggling with his technique. I remember getting a letter from an old archer who had shot the bow for more than fifty years. He was past seventy and had to resort to a thirty-five pound weapon. He complained that his release was faulty, but he felt that with a little more practice he could perfect his loose and make a perfect shot. Since writing he has entered the Happy Hunting Grounds, still a trifle off in form.

Even a sylvan archer needs to practice form at the targets. He should study the game from its scientific principles as formulated by Horace Ford, the greatest target shot ever known.

The point-of-aim system and target practice improve one's hunting. Hunting, on the other hand, spoils one's target work. The use of heavy bows so accustoms the muscles to gross reactions that they fail to adjust themselves to the finer requirements of light bows and to the precise technique of the target range.

The field archer gets his practice by going out in the open and shooting at marks of any sort, at all distances, from five to two hundred yards. A bush, a stray piece of paper, a flower, a shadow on the grass, all are objects for his shafts.

The open heath, shaded forest, hills and dales, all make good grounds. As he comes over a knoll a bush on the farther side represents a deer, he shoots instantly. He must learn to run, to stop short and shoot, fresh or weary he must be able to draw his bow and discharge one arrow after another. With the bow unstrung walking along the trail, often we have stopped at the word of command, strung the bow, drawn an arrow from the quiver, nocked it, and discharged it within the space of five seconds. Deliberation, however, is much more desirable.

Let several archers go into the fields together and roam over the land, aiming at various marks; it makes for robust and accurate game shooting.

Shooting an exact line is much easier than getting the exact length. For this reason it is easier to split the willow wand at sixty or eighty yards than it seems.

Often we have tried this feat to amuse ourselves or our friends, and seldom more than six arrows are needed to strike such a lath or stick at this distance. Hitting objects tossed in the air is not so difficult either. A small tin can or box thrown fifteen or twenty feet upward at a distance of ten or fifteen yards can be hit nearly every time, especially if the archer waits until it just reaches the apex of its course and shoots when it is practically stationary.

Shooting at swinging objects helps to train one in leading running or flying game.

Turtle shooting, that form in which the arrow is discharged directly upward and is supposed to drop on the mark, is difficult and attended with few hits, but it trains one in estimating wind drift.

An archer should also learn the elevation or trajectory at which his arrows fly at various distances. Shooting in the woods over hanging limbs may interfere with a good shot. In this case the archer can kneel and thus lower his flight to avoid interception.

In kneeling it seems that the right knee should be on the ground, while the left foot is forward. This is a natural pose to assume during walking, and the left thigh should be held out of the way of the bow-string. When not in use, but braced, the bow should be carried in the left hand, the string upward, the tip pointing forward. It never should be swung about like a club nor shouldered like a gun.

Shooting from horseback is not impossible, but it must be done off the left side of the horse, and a certain amount of practice is necessary for the horse as well as for the archer.

It is surprising how accurately one can shoot at night. Even the dimmest outline will serve the bowman, and his shaft has an uncanny way of finding the mark.

When it comes to missing the mark, that is the subject for a sad story. It takes an inveterate optimist to stand the moral strain of persistent missing. In fact, it is this that spoils the archery career of many a tyro—he gives up in despair. It looks so easy, but really is so difficult to hit the mark. But do not be cast down, keep eternally at practice, and ultimately you will be rewarded. Nothing stands a man in such good stead in this matter as to have started shooting in his youth.

And do not imagine that we are infallible in our shooting. Some of the most humiliating moments of our lives have come through poor shooting. Just when we wanted to do our best, before an expectant gathering, we have done our most stupid missing. But even this has its compensations and inures us to defeat.

It is a striking fact that we shoot better when confronted by the game itself. Under actual hunting conditions you will hit closer to your point than on the target field.

Study every move for clean, accurate shooting, and analyze your failures so that you can correct your faults. Extreme care and utmost effort will be rewarded by greater accuracy.

Other things being equal, it is the man who shoots with his heart in his bow that hits the mark.

IX

THE PRINCIPLES OP HUNTING

In the early dawn of life man took up weapons against the beasts about him. With club, ax, spear, knife, and sling he protected himself or sought his game. To strike at a distance, he devised the bow. With the implements of the chase he has won his way in the world.

Today there is no need to battle with the beasts of prey and little necessity to kill wild animals for food; but still the hunting instinct persists. The love of the chase still thrills us and all the misty past echoes with the hunter's call.

In the joy of hunting is intimately woven the love of the great outdoors. The beauty of woods, valleys, mountains, and skies feeds the soul of the sportsman where the quest of game only whets his appetite.

After all, it is not the killing that brings satisfaction, it is the contest of skill and cunning. The true hunter counts his achievement in proportion to the effort involved and the fairness of the sport.

With the rapid development of firearms, hunting tends to lose its sporting quality. The killing of game is becoming too easy; there is little triumph and less glory than in the days of yore. Game preservation demands a limitation of armament. We should do well to abandon the more powerful and accurate implements of destruction, and revert to the bow.

Here we have a weapon of beauty and romance. He who shoots with a bow, puts his life's energy into it. The force behind the flying shaft must be placed there by the archer. At the moment of greatest strain he must draw every sinew to the utmost; his hand must be steady; his nerves under absolute control; his eye keen and clear. In the hunt he pits his well-trained skill against the instinctive cunning of his quarry. By the most adroit cleverness, he must approach within striking distance, and when he speeds his low whispering shaft and strikes his game, he has won by the strength of arm and nerve. It is a noble sport.

However, not all temperaments are suited to archery. There must be something within the deeper memories of his inheritance to which the bow appeals. A mere passing fancy will not suffice to make him an archer. It is the unusual person who will overcome the early difficulties and persevere with the bow through love of it.

The real archer when he goes afield enters a land of subtle delight. The dew glistens on the leaves, the thrush sings in the bush, the soft wind blows, and all nature welcomes him as she has the hunter since the world began. With his bow in his hand, his arrows softly rustling in the quiver, a horn at his back, and a hound at his heels, what more can a man want in life?

In America our hearts have heard the low whistle of the flying arrow and the sweet hum of the bowstring singing in the book, *The Witchery of Archery* by Maurice

Thompson. To Will and Maurice Thompson we owe a debt of gratitude hard to pay. The tale of their sylvan exploits in the everglades of Florida has a charm that borders on the fay. We who shoot the bow today are children of their fantasy, offspring of their magic. As the parents of American archery, we offer them homage and honor.

Ernest Thompson Seton is another patron of archery to whom all who have read *Two Little Savages* must be eternally grateful. Not only has he given us a reviving touch of the outdoors, but he puts the bow and arrow in its true setting, a background of nature.

When Arthur Young, Will Compton, and I began hunting with the bow, we wrote Will Thompson to join us. Because he is such a commanding figure in the history of our craft, I think it proper to quote from one of his letters:

"MY DEAR DR. POPE:

"The *Sunset Magazine* containing your charming account of Ishi and your hunting adventures, and the bunch of photographs of the transfixed deer, quail, and rabbits came duly, and are mine, now, tomorrow, and for life. You were very fortunate to have won your archery triumphs where you could photograph them. I would give much indeed if I could have photos of the scenes of my brother's and my successes in the somber and game-thronged wilds of the gloomy Okefinokee Swamp. I think I sent you long ago the two numbers of *Forest and Stream* in which the history of that most wonderful of all my outings appeared. If I did not do so I will loan you the only copy I have. Let me know.

"I am glad, so glad, that you young athletic men are following the wild trails armed with the most romantic weapon man ever fashioned, and I would give almost any precious thing I hold to fare with you once to the game land of your choice, and to watch and wait by a slender trail while you and your young, strong comrades stole through the secret haunts of the wild things, and to listen to the faint footfalls of the coming deer, roused by your entrance into their secret lairs. To see the soft and devious approach of the wary thing; to see the lifted light head turned sharply back toward the evil that roused it from its bed of ferns; to feel the strong bow tightening in my hand as the thin, hard string comes back; to feel the leap of the loosened cord, the jar of the bow, and see the long streak of the going shaft, and hear the almost sickening 'chuck' of the stabbing arrow. No one can know how I have loved the woods, the streams, the trails of the wild, the ways of the things of slender limbs, of fine nose, of great eager ears, of mild wary eyes, and of vague and half-revealed forms and colors. I have been their friend and mortal enemy. I have so loved them that I longed to kill them. But I gave them far more than a fair chance.

"How many I have missed to one I have killed! How often the fierce arrow hissed its threat close by the wide ears! How often the puff of lifted feathers has marked the innocuous passage of my very best arrow! How often the roar of wings has replied to the 'chuck' of my steel-head shaft as it stabbed the tree branch under the grouse's feet! *Oh, le bon temps, que de siècle de fer.*

"Let me know whether I sent you *Deep in Okefinokee Swamp.* I enclose you a little poem published long ago in *Forest and Stream* and picked up by the *Literary Digest* and other periodicals. You will, I think, feel the love of the bow, and the outdoors, as well as the great cry for the lost brother running through the long sob that pervades it.

"Send me anything you publish, for I know I should be pleased. Love to you and a handgrasp to your comrade archers.

"WILL THOMPSON."

After the Civil War, where both youths fought in the Confederate Army and Maurice was wounded, they returned to their Southern home, broken in health, reduced in circumstances, and deprived of firearms by Government restrictions. They turned to the bow and hunting as naturally as a boy turns to play. Out of their experiences we have a lyric of exquisite purity, *The Witchery of Archery*.

As a result of the interest stimulated by the recount of their exploits, the National Archery Association was established and held its first tournament at Chicago in the year 1879. It has ever since nurtured the sport and furthered competitive enthusiasm.

Maurice later became a noted author, Will an attorney-at-law, the dean of American archers and a poet of remarkably happy expression. Here I feel at liberty to insert one of Will Thompson's verses, sent me in personal communications:

AN ARROW SONG

A song from green Floridian vales I heard,
Soft as the sea-moan when the waves are slow;
Sweeter than melody of brook or bird,
Keener than any winds that breathe or blow;
A magic music out of memory stirred,
A strain that charms my heart to overflow
With such vast yearning that my eyes are blurred.
Oh, song of dreams, that I no more shall know!
Bewildering carol without spoken word!
Faint as a stream's voice murmuring under snow,
Sad as a love forevermore deferred,
Song of the arrow from the Master's bow,
Sung in Floridian vales long, long ago.
WILL H. THOMPSON.

A memory of my brother Maurice.

The Thompsons devoted much of their bow shooting to birds. Not only did they hunt, but they studied the abundant avian life of the Florida coast.

An archer must always, perforce, study animate nature and learn its ways before he can capture it. In our early training with Ishi, the Indian, he taught us to look before he taught us to shoot. "Little bit walk, too much look," was his motto. The roving eye and the light step are the signs of the forest voyageur.

The ideal way for an archer to travel is to carry on his shoulders a knapsack containing a light sleeping bag and enough food to last him a week. With me this means coffee, tea, sugar, canned milk, dried fruit, rice, cornmeal, flour and baking powder mixture, a little bacon, butter, and seasoning. This will weigh less than ten pounds. With other minor appurtenances in the ditty bag, including an arrow-repairing kit, one's burden is less than twenty pounds, an easy load.

If you have a dog, make him carry his own dry meal in little saddle-bags on his back, as Dan Beard suggests. Then, with two dozen arrows in your quiver, and your bow, the open trail lies ahead. There is always meat to be had for the shooting. The camp fire and your dog are companions at night, and at dawn all the world rolls out before you as you go. It is a happy life!

When Ishi started to shoot with me, one bowman after another appeared on the scene to join us. Among the first came Will Compton, a man of mature years and many experiences. Brought up on the plains, he learned to shoot the bow with the Sioux Indians. As a boy of fourteen he shot his first deer with an arrow. From that time on, deer, elk, antelope, birds of all sorts, and even buffalo fell before this primitive weapon. He later hunted with the gun until the very ease of killing turned him against it. So when he came to us, he was a seasoned archer. Upon a visit to a Japanese archery gallery in the Panama-Pacific Exposition he met for the first time Arthur Young, also an expert hunter with the gun. A friendship sprang up between them, and Compton taught Young to shoot the bow.

Compton had worked in the shop of Barnes, the bowmaker of Forest Grove, Oregon, and later he went into the Cascade Mountains and cut yew staves with an idea of selling them to the English bowyers. The Great War of 1914 prevented this, and so we had an unlimited supply of yew wood for use.

We three gravitated together and shot with Ishi until his last sickness and departure. Then our serious work began. We found it not only a delightful way of hunting, but a trio makes success more certain in the field.

In California there is an abundance of game; small animals exist everywhere and there is no better training than to stalk the wary ground squirrel or the alert cottontail. These every archer should school himself to hit before he ventures after larger beasts.

Infinite patience and practice are needed to make a hunter. He must earn his right to take life by the painful effort of constant shooting.

We shot together, and many are the bags of game we filled. We discovered in the humble ground squirrel a delectable morsel more palatable than chicken; re-discovered it, we may say, because the Indian knew it first. In killing these little pests we take to the open fields, approach a burrow by creeping up a gully or dip in the land, rise up and shoot at such distances as we can. I recall one day when Young and I got twenty-four squirrels with the bow. Upon another occasion Young by himself secured seventeen in one morning; the last five were killed with five successive arrows, the last squirrel being forty-two paces away.

Rabbits are best hunted in company. Here the startled rodent skips briskly off, down his accustomed run, only to meet another archer standing motionless, ready with his arrow.

It seems legitimate with this rudimentary weapon to shoot animals on the stand, or set, a sporting permit not granted to the devotee of the shotgun, who has a hundred chances to our one.

We found from the very first that the arrow was more humane than the gun. Counting all hunters, for every animal brought home with the gun, whether duck, quail, or deer, at least two are hit and die in pain in the brush.

Just to illustrate this, Mr. Young reported to me the results of his shooting with a small rifle at ground squirrels. So expert is he that to hit a squirrel in any spot but the head is quite unusual. In one day's shooting between himself and his young son, they hit thirty-six animals, sixteen of these escaped and disappeared down their burrows, there to die later of their wounds.

With the arrow it is different. Not only is the destructive power as great as a small bullet, but the shaft holds the animal so that it cannot escape. Practically none are lost in our hunts. A strange phenomenon is seen in larger animals; they are easier to kill with an arrow than small ones. A shot in either the chest or abdominal cavity of a deer is invariably fatal in a few minutes; while a rabbit may carry an arrow off until the obstructing undergrowth checks his flight. It seems that their vital areas and blood vessels being smaller, are less readily injured by the missile. A bullet can crash into the brain of an animal, tear out a mass of tissue and generally shatter his structure, but cause little bleeding. An arrow wound is clean-cut and the hemorrhage is tremendous, but if not immediately fatal, it heals readily and does little harm. The pain is no greater with the arrow than with the bullet.

Our hunting of squirrel and rabbits was merely preparatory to the taking of larger game; but even on our more pretentious expeditions, we fill the vacant hours with lesser shooting and fill the camp kettle with sweet tidbits.

Many a quail, partridge, sage hen, or grouse has flown from the heather into our bag transfixed by a feathered shaft. Both Compton and Young have shot ducks and geese, some on the wing. But we cannot compete with the experiences of Maurice Thompson who, shooting ninety-eight arrows, landed sixteen ducks on the wing.

Some amusing incidents have occurred in bird shooting. We consider the bluejay a legitimate mark any day; he is a rascal of the deepest dye, so we always shoot at him.

Compton once tried one of his long shots at a jay on the ground nearly eighty yards off. His line was good, but his shot fell short. The arrow skidded and struck the bird in the tail just as he left the ground for flight. The two rose together and sailed off into space, like an aeroplane, with a preposterously long rudder, the arrow out behind. They slowly wheeled in a circle a hundred yards in diameter when the bird, nearing the archer, fell exhausted at his feet. Compton picked up the jay, drew the arrow from the shallow skin wound above his tail, and tossed him in the air. He disappeared with a volley of expletives.

With an arrow it is also possible to shoot fish. Many wise old trout, incurious and contented, deep in the shadowed pool, have been coaxed to the frying pan through the archer's skill. Well I recall once, how shooting fish not only brought us meat, but changed our luck. Young and I were on a bear hunt. It had been a long, weary and unsuccessful quest of the elusive beast. Bears seemed to have become extinct, so we took to shooting trout in a quiet little meadow stream. Having buried an arrow in the far bank, with a short run and a leap Young cleared the brook and landed on the greensward beyond. The succulent turf slipped beneath his feet and, like an acrobat, the archer turned a back somersault into the cold mountain water. Bow, clattering arrows, camera, field glasses and man, all sank beneath the limpid surface. With a shout of laughter he clambered to the bank, his faithful bow still in his hand, his quiver empty of arrows, but full of water. After a hasty salvage of all damaged goods, we journeyed along, no worse for the wetting. But immediately we began to see bear signs and ultimately got our bruin. Young later said that if he had known the change of luck that went with a good ducking, he would have tried it sooner.

We have often been asked if we do not poison our arrow points. Most people seem to have the idea that an arrow is too impotent to cause death; they conceive it a refined sort of torture and have no conception of its destructive nature.

It is true that we thought at first of putting poison on our arrows intended for lions, and we did coat some broad-heads with mucilage and powdered strychnine, but we never used them. My physiologic experiments with curare, the South American arrow poison, aconitin, the Japanese Ainu poison, and buffogen, the Central American poison, had convinced me that strychnine was more deadly. It would not harm the meat in the dilution obtained in the blood, and it was cheap and effective.

Buffogen is obtained by the natives by taking the tropical toad, Buffo Nigra, enclosing it in a segment of bamboo, heating this over a slow fire and gathering the exuded juice of the dessicated batrachian. It is a very powerful substance, having an action similar to that of adrenalin and strychnine.

Salamandrine, an extract obtained from the macerated skin of the common red water-dog, is also violently toxic.

But we had a disgust for these things. We soon learned, moreover, that our arrows were sufficient without these adjuncts, and we deemed it unsportsmanlike to consider them. Therefore, we abandoned the idea.

Ishi knew of the employment of these killing substances, but he did not use them. In his tribe they made a poison by teasing a rattlesnake and having it strike a piece of deer's liver. This was later buried in the ground until it rotted, and the arrow points were smeared with this revolting material. It was a combination of crotalin venom and ptomaine poisons, a very deadly mess.

We much prefer the bright, clean knife-blade of our broad-heads to any other missile.

The principles involved in seeking game with the bow and arrow are those of the still hunt, only more refined.

An archer's striking distance extends from ten to one hundred yards. For small animals it lies between ten and forty; for large game from forty to eighty or a hundred. The distance at which most small game flush varies with the country in which they live, the nature of their enemies, and the prevalence of hunters. Quail and rabbits usually will permit a man to approach them within twenty or thirty yards. This they have learned is a safe distance for a fox or wildcat who must hurl himself at them. It is quite a fair distance for any man with any weapon, particularly the bow.

Most small game, especially rabbits, have sufficient curiosity to stand after their first startled retreat. Beneath a bush or clump of weeds they squat and watch on the *qui vive*. The arrow may find them there when it strikes, but often the very flash of its departure and the quick movement of the hand send the little beastie flying to his cover. Here two sportsmen working together succeed better; one attracts the rabbit's attention, the other shoots the shot.

The marmot or woodchuck, is an impudent and cautious animal and he is a difficult mark for a bowman's aim. But nothing has more comic situations than an afternoon spent in a ground-hog village. After an incontinent scuttle to his burrow, an old warrior backs into his hole, then brazenly lifts his head and fastens his glittering eye upon you. The contest of quickness then begins; the archer and the marmot play shoot and dodge until one after the other all the arrows are exhausted or a hit is registered. The ground-hog never quits. I can recall one strenuous noon hour in an outcropping of rock where, between shattered arrows, precipitous chasing of transfixed old warriors, defiant whistlers on all sides, we piled up nearly a dozen victims.

Quail hunting requires careful shooting, but it is good training for the bowman. A sentinel cock, sitting on a low limb, warns his covey of our approach, but he himself makes a gallant mark for the archer. I saw Compton spit such a bird on his arrow at fifty yards, while a confused scurrying flock made easy shooting for two hunters. I am ashamed to say that we have often taken advantage of the evening roosting of these birds in trees to secure a supper for ourselves.

But the archer must exercise caution in this team work in the brush. He should never forget that an arrow will kill a man as readily as it does an animal and that one should always consider where his shot ultimately will land, both for the purpose of finding his shaft and avoiding accidents. Arrows have a great habit of glancing. Once when hunting quail in a patch of willow in a dry wash, Compton shot at a bird on a branch, missed it, and at the same instant Young, who was on the opposite side of the thicket, heard a thwack at his right and turned to find a broad-head arrow buried up to the barbs in a willow limb just the height of the heart. It gave us all pause for thought. Look before you shoot!

While small game may be taken by tactics of moderate cunning, larger and more wary animals must be hunted by artful measures. Deer, still abundant in our land, and properly safeguarded by game laws, test the woodsman's skill to the utmost. To learn the art of finding deer, or successful approach and ultimate capture, one must study life in the open. Let him read the work of Van Dyke on still-hunting to gain some idea of the many problems entailed.

In our country we have the Columbia black tail deer. Of course, only bucks should be shot; as an old forest ranger said to me, "Does ain't deer." And no one but a starving man would shoot a fawn. Here bucks are hunted only in the fall, just as they shed their velvet and before the rutting season. At this time they keep pretty quiet in the brush or seek the higher lookout points on mountain ridges. They browse mostly at night and are to be met wandering to water or back to their beds. The older ones lie very quietly and seldom move far from their cover. Sometimes in the heat of the day they stir about or go to drink. The younger bucks are more audacious and seem to feel that their wisdom and strength can carry them anywhere. For this reason a two-year-old or forked horn is much more frequently brought down.

It is interesting to note that even in this day of civilization and the extinction of wild life, deer are to be found within a radius of twenty miles from our largest cities in California. We, however, invariably journey by rail or motor car from fifty to three hundred miles to do most of our hunting. We seek those regions that are most primeval. Here game is largely in an undisturbed condition. From some station or outpost we pack with horses into the foothills or higher levels of the Coast Range or Sierra Nevada Mountains. Having made camp in a sheltered spot, we hunt on foot over the adjacent country.

Just at dawn and at sunset are the favorite times for finding deer.

The hunters rise from their sleeping bags, make a hasty meal of coffee and cakes, and long before the light of dawn sweeps the eastern sky, they must be on the trail. Silently and alert they enter the land of suspected deer. Taking advantage of every bit of cover, traveling into the wind where possible, looking at every shadow, every spot of moving color, they advance. Where trails exist they follow these, or if the ground be carpeted with soft pine needles, they flit between the deeper shades of the forest, watchful, and hearing every woodland sound.

Often the crashing bound of a deer through the brush proves that cautious though the archer may be, more cautious is the deer. Or having seen him first, the archer crouches, advances to a favorable spot, gauges the distance, clears his eye, and nerves himself for a supreme effort. He draws his sturdy bow till the sharpened barb pricks his finger and bids him loose—a hit, a leap, a clattering flight. Watching and immovable, the archer listens with straining ears. He must not stir, he must not follow; later he can trail the quarry. Give the wounded deer time to lie down and die, then find him.

It is a surprising experience to see animals stand and let arrows fall about them without fear. An archer has special privileges because he uses nature's tools.

The whizzing missile is no more than a passing bird to the beast. What hurt can that bring? The quiet man is only an interesting object on the landscape, there is no noise to cause alarm. Most animals are ruled by curiosity till fright takes control. But some are less curious than others, notably the turkey. There is a story among sportsmen that describes this in the Indian's speech. "Deer see Injun. Deer say, 'I see Injun; no, him stump; no, him Injun; no, maybe stump.' Injun shoot. Turkey see Injun; he say, 'I see Injun.' He go!"

The use of dogs in deer hunting should be restricted to trailing wounded animals. Here a little mongrel, if properly trained, serves better than a blooded breed. No dog should be permitted to run deer, especially if wounded. It is only the dog's nose we need, not his legs. An ideal canine for an archer would be one having the olfactory organs of a hound and the reasoning capacity of a college professor. With him one could trail animals, yet not flush them; perceive the imminence of game, yet not startle it; run coyotes, wolves, cougars, and bear, yet never confuse their scent nor abandon the quest of one for that of another. But as it is, no dog seems capable of doing all things, so we need specialists. A good bear and lion dog should never taste deer meat nor follow his tracks.

A good coon dog should stick to coons and let rabbits alone. And the sort of dog an archer needs for deer is one that can point them, yet will not follow one unless it is wounded.

Every good dog will come to the ringing note of the horn.

And after all, there lies the soul of the sport. The fragrance of the earth, the deep purple valleys, the wooded mountain slopes, the clean sweet wind, the mysterious murmur of the tree tops, all call the hunter forth. When he hears the horn and the baying hound his heart leaps within him, he grasps his good yew bow, girds his quiver on his hip, and enters a world of romance and adventure.

X

THE RACCOON, WILDCAT, FOX, COON, CAT, AND WOLF

Of all the canny beasts, Brother Coon is the wisest, and were it not for his imprudence and self-assurance, he would be less frequently captured than the coyote, who is also a very clever gentleman. As it is, a raccoon hunt is a nocturnal escapade that may be enjoyed by any lively boy or man who happens to own a coon dog.

Now a coon dog is any sort of a dog that has a sporting instinct and a large propensity for combat. We have, of course, that product of culture and breeding, the coon hound, an offshoot from the English fox hound. This dog is a marvel in his own sphere.

Although we have not devoted a great deal of time to coon hunting, one or another of our group has counted the scalps of quite a number of *Procyon lotor*. Having been accepted as a companion of one or two or more ambitious and enthusiastic dogs, we start out at dusk to hunt the creek bottoms for coons. Provided with bows, blunt arrows, and a lantern, we unleash the dogs, and the fun begins.

One must be prepared to scramble through blackberry vines, nettles, tangled swamps, and to climb trees. The dogs busy themselves sniffing and working through the underbrush, crossing the creek back and forth, investigating old hollow trees, displaying signs of exaggerated interest and industry.

Suddenly there is a change in their vocal expression. Heretofore the short, snappy bark has spoken only of anticipation and eagerness; now there comes the instinctive yelp of the questing beast, the hound on the scent. It bursts from them like a wail from the distant past. As if shot, they are off in a bunch. A clatter of sounds, scratching, rustling, and scrambling, we hear them tearing through the brush. We follow, but are soon outdistanced. Down the creek bed we go, splash through mud, clamber over logs, stop, listen, and hear them baying, afar off. Their voices rise in a chorus, some are high-pitched, incessant yelps, some are deep-voiced, bell-like tones. We know they have him treed and, breathless, we push forward, arriving in the order of our physical vigor, those with the best legs and lungs coming first.

High up in a tree, out on a limb, we see a shadowy form and two glowing orbs—that is the coon. The dogs are insistent; since they cannot climb, although they try, man must rout the victim out. Somebody turns a flashlight on the varmint. Frank Ferguson is the champion coon hunter; so he draws a blunt arrow from his quiver, takes quick aim and shoots. A dull thud tells that he has hit, but the coon does not fall. Another arrow whistles past, registering a miss; then a sharp click as the blunt point of the third arrow strikes the creature's head, a stifled snarl, a falling body, a rush of dogs on the ground, and all is over. The hounds are delighted, and we count one chicken thief the less.

Sometimes the coon becomes the aggressor. He boldly enters our camp at night and purloins a savory ham or rifles the larder and eats a pound of butter. He fully deserves what is coming to him. I loose Teddy and Dixie, my two faithful hounds. The morning mist is rising from the stream, the tree trunks are barely visible in the early dawn, the grasses drip with dew.

The eager dogs take up the trail and start on a run up the stream bank. They cross on a great fallen tree and mount the wooded hill on the other side where I lose them in the jungle. I run on by instinct, listening for their directing bark. Once in a while I catch it faintly in the distance. They must be mounting rapidly and too busy to bark. Again it is audible far off to my left and I force my tired legs to renewed energy, climbing higher and higher.

Up I mount through the forest, alert for the telltale yelp. There it is, a whine and faint, stifled guttural sounds, but so indistinct and so obscured by the prattle of the stream and the murmuring tree tops that I fail to locate it. So I flounder on through vines and underbrush, wondering where my dogs have gone. I blow the horn and Dixie answers with a pathetic howl, away off to the right. I run and blow the horn again; again that puppy whine. Teddy doesn't answer and I wonder how Dixie could have been lost, though after all, he is only a recent graduate from the kennel and unseasoned in this world of canine misery and wisdom. Unexpectedly, I come upon him, looking very disconsolate and somewhat mauled. There is no doubt about it, he has rushed in where angels fear to tread. He has received a recent lesson in coon hunting. So I console him with a little petting and ask him where is Teddy. Just then I hear a subterranean gurgle and scuffle and rushing off to a nearby clump of trees, I find that away down under the ground in a hollow stump, there is a death struggle going on—Teddy and the coon are having it out. From the sounds I know that Ted has him by the throat and is waiting for the end. But he seems very weak himself. As I shout down the hole to encourage him, the coon, with one final effort, wrests himself free from the dog and comes scuttling out of the hole. With undignified haste I back away from the outlet and fumble a blunt arrow on the string, and I am just in time, for here comes one of the maddest and one of the sickest coons I ever saw. With a hasty shot back of the ear, I bowl him over and put him out of his misery. Turning him over with my foot to make sure he is finished, I note how desperate the fight must have been. His neck and brisket are a mass of mangled flesh and skin. Then reaching deep down in the hole I grab poor exhausted Teddy by the scruff of his neck, lift him out, and let him regain his breath in the fresh air. He certainly is a weary champion. The coon has bitten him viciously between the legs and along the abdomen. After a while we all go down to the stream and there bathe the wounded heroes.

With the rascally old coon over my shoulder, we three wander back to camp in time for congratulations and wonderment of the children and the consolation of hot victuals.

That is a typical coon hunt with us. Some are less damaging to the dogs, but usually this little cousin of the bears is able to give a good account of himself in the contest.

Ferguson and his pack of fox terriers have had more experience with the redoubtable raccoon than the rest of us; he hunts them for their pelts. He is also a trapper for the market and long since has found that the blunt arrow shot from a light bow serves very admirably for dispatching the captured varmint when once trapped.

The fox is more difficult to meet in the wilds. His business hours are also at night, but he extends them not infrequently both into the sunrise and twilight zones. One of the most beautiful sights I ever witnessed came unexpectedly while hunting deer.

It was evening; dusky shadows merged all objects into a common drab. Two silent, graceful foxes rose over the crest of a little eminence of ground before me. Outlined distinctly against a red dirt bank across the ravine, they stood just for a moment in surprise. I drew my bow and instantly loosed an arrow at the foremost. It flew swift as a night-hawk and with a rush of wind passed his head. As is usual at dusk, I had overestimated the distance. It was but forty yards; I thought it fifty.

Half-startled, but not alarmed, the two foxes fixed their gaze upon me a second, then gracefully, and with infinite ease, they cleared a three-foot bush without a run and disappeared in the gloom.

But in that leap I gained all the thrill that I missed with my arrow. Such facile grace I never saw. Without an effort they rose, hovered an instant in midair, straightened their wonderful bushy tails as an aeroplane readjusts its flight, and soared level across the obstacle. One final downward curve of that beautiful counterbalance landed them smoothly on the distant side of the bush where, with uninterrupted speed, they vanished from sight. For the first time I appreciated why a fox has such a light, long, fluffy caudal appendage. Marvelous!

Often at night when coming late to camp through the woods, a fox has emerged from the outer sphere of darkness and given a querulous little bark at me. Wheeling with a bright light on the head, I could have shot him, but then he is such a harmless little denizen of the woods that I hate to kill him. But after all, is he really harmless? The little culprit! He actually does a deal of harm, destroying birds' nests, eating the young, catching quail and rabbits—I don't know that we should spare him.

With horses and hounds we have chased many foxes over the sage and chaparral-covered hills.

The fox terrier and the black and tan are excellent dogs for this sort of work. These little hunters are keen for the sport and make their way beneath the brush where a larger dog follows with difficulty. With strident yelps the pack picks up the hot trail, and off they rush, helter skelter, through the sage and chaparral; we circle and cross cut, dash down the draw, traverse the open forest meadow and follow the furious procession into the trees.

There the hard-pressed little fox makes a final spurt for a large red pine, leaps straight for the bare trunk, mounts like a squirrel and gains a rotten limb, panting with effort. As we approach he climbs still higher and lodges himself securely in the crotch of the tree, gazing furtively down at the dogs.

Who ever thought that a fox could climb such a tree! It was twenty feet to the first foothold on a decayed branch; yet there he was, and we saw him do it.

Sometimes when the fleeing fox has mounted a smaller tree, we have shaken him from his perch and let the dogs deal with him as they think best—for a dog must not be too often cheated of his conquest or he loses heart. Sometimes we have mounted the tree and slipped a noose over the fox's neck, brought him close, tied his wicked little jaws tightly together with a thong, packed him off on the horse to show him to the children in camp, and later given him his liberty. Or, as in the case of our little villain up the pine tree, we have drawn a careful arrow and settled his life problems with a broad-head.

In winter time the trap and the blunt arrow add another fur collar to the coat of the feminine sybarite.

The woods and plains are full of hunters. The hawk is on the wing; the murderous mink and weasel never cease their crimes; the bird seeks the slothful worm and jumping insect; the fox, cat, and wolf forever quest for food. And so we, hunting in the early morning light, once saw a flock of quail flushed long before our presence should have given them cause for flight. Compton and Young, arrows nocked and muscles taut, crept cautiously to the thicket of wild roses out of which flew the quail. There, stooping low, they saw the spotted legs of a lynx softly stalking the birds. Aiming above the legs where surely there must be a body, Young sped an arrow. There was a thud, a snarl, and an animal tore through the crackling bushes. Out from the other side bounded the cat, and there, not twenty yards off, he met Compton. Like a flash another arrow flew at him, flew through him, and down he tumbled, a flurry of scratching claws, torn up grasses and dust. Young's arrow, having been a blunt barbed head, still lodged in his chest, and as the lynx succumbed to death I took his picture.

Lazy, sleepy cat, both lynx and wildcats, we meet not infrequently on our travels. Still they are ever up to mischief in spite of their indolent casual appearance. Often have we seen them slink out from a bunch of cover, cross the open hillside, and there, if within range, receive an archer's salute. Many times we miss them, sometimes we hit; but that's not the point, we are not so anxious to get them as to send greetings.

Then, too, since Ishi taught us to do it, we have called these wary creatures from the thicket and sometimes got a shot.

With the dogs, the story is soon told and the rôle of the bowman is without triumph; so for this reason, we prefer the accidental meetings and impromptu adventures to the more certain contact. Still when at night we hear the tingling call of the lynx up in the woods, we yearn for a willing dog and a taut bowstring.

With the distant barking wail of the prairie wolf or coyote, one feels differently. I presume that man has become so accustomed to the dog that he has rather a kindly feeling toward this little brother of the plains, called by the Aztecs coyote, or "wild one." We know his evil propensities and his economic menace, but still we love him, or at least, look upon him much as the Indians do, as a sort of comedian among animals.

Ishi used to tell me of his laughable experiences with coyotes. When coming home at night with a haunch of venison on his shoulder, a band of these gamins of the wilds would follow him teasing at his heels. Ishi would turn upon them with feigned fury and chase them back into the shadows or wield his bow as a short lance and jab them vigorously in the ribs—when he could.

With him the coyote was the reincarnation of a mythical character, half buffoon, half magician. He was cunning, crafty, humorous, and evil, all in one, and no doings of the animal folk ever progressed very far without the entrance of the "coyote doctor" on the scene. He was the doer of tricks and caster of spells, but still he himself met with misadventure—witness how he lost his claws. Of course, he had long claws like the bear in the beginning, and fine silky fur. But one night, coming weary from hunting and cold, he crept into a hollow oak gall to sleep. The wind fanned the embers of the camp-fire and the dry grass burst into a blaze. It swept up to the sleeping coyote, where only his feet protruded from his hollow spherical den. Here they hung out for lack of room. So, of course, his claws were burned off before the pain wakened him. He leaped out of his nest, dashed through the blaze, and plunged into the creek, not in time, however, to keep his beautiful long hair from being singed. Even to this day he has that half-scorched, moth-eaten pelt, and his claws are only those of a coyote.

When met in the open, the prairie wolf seems so weary and listless. If at a distance, he protests at your entrance upon his domain with a forlorn wail, or insolently stares at you from a ridge. He sits and looks or moves about dyspeptically waiting for you to go.

Once I remember that we saw one sitting on his haunches a hundred and eighty yards away. Compton loosed an arrow at him, one of those whining, complaining shafts that drone through the air. The coyote heard it coming; he pricked up his ears, pointed his nose skyward, rose and limped lively to the left, turned, peered into the sky, and ran a short distance to the right, then loped off just in time to be missed by the descending arrow, which landed exactly where he sat originally. It was indeed a most ludicrous performance, incidentally a splendid shot.

Just as with a rifle, the coyote simply is not there when your missile strikes. He doesn't seem to bestir himself greatly, but just seems to drag himself out of harm's way at the last moment. How often have we let fly at him, sometimes at a group of them, but seldom has he been hit. A beginner's luck seems to fool him, however. One of our neophytes with the bow, having had his tackle less than a month, was out riding in his new automobile in company with a group of friends. The bow at that time was his vade-mecum; he never left it home. He chanced to see a stray coyote near the side of the highway when, after passing it a hundred yards or so, he stopped his machine, grabbed his trusty weapon, which he had hardly learned to shoot, strung it, nocked an arrow, and ran back to take a shot at the animal in question. His eagerness and obvious incapacity so amused the gay company in the machine, that they cheered him on with laughter and ridicule.

Undaunted, our bowman hastened back, saw the crafty beast retreating in a slinking gallop, drew his faithful bow, and shot at sixty yards. Unerringly the fatal shaft flew, struck the coyote back of the ear and laid him low without a quiver.

Mad with unexpected triumph, our archer dragged his slain victim back to the car to meet the jeering company, and confounded them with his success. Loud were the shouts of joy; a war dance ensued to celebrate the great event. When done the merry party cranked up the machine and sped on its fragrant way, a happier and a more enlightened bevy of children.

Thus is shown the danger of utter innocence.

These chance meetings seem rather unlucky for coyotes. Frank Ferguson, when trapping in the foothills of the Sierras, repeatedly had his traps robbed by an impudent member of the wolf family. One day while making his regular rounds and approaching a set, he saw in the distance a coyote run off with the catch of his trap. Seeing that the wolf turned up a branch creek, Ferguson cut across the intervening neck of the woods to intercept him if possible. He reached the stream bottom at the moment the coyote came trotting past. Having a blunt arrow on the bowstring, he shot across the twenty-five yards of bank, and quite unexpectedly cracked the animal on the foreleg, breaking the bone. A jet of blood spurted out with astonishing force, and the brute staggered for a space of time. This gave Ferguson a moment to nock a second shaft, a broad-head, and with that accuracy known to come in excitement, he drove it completely through the animal's body, killing it instantly. When next we met after this episode, he showed me the bloody arrows and wolf skin as mute evidence of his skill.

Ferguson was won over to archery when, as packer upon our first trip together, he asked Compton to show him what could be done with the bow in the way of accurate shooting. Compton is particularly good at long ranges, so he pointed out a bush about one hundred and seventy-five yards distant. It was about the size of a dog. Compton took unusual care with his shots, and dropped three successive arrows in that bush. When "Ferg" saw this he took the bow seriously.

The timber wolf is seldom met in our clime, and so for this reason he has been spared the fate common to all fearsome beasts that cross the trail of an archer. But with that fateful hope which has foreshadowed and seemingly insured our subsequent achievement, I fervently wish that some day we may meet, wolf and bowman.

In the absence of this the more austere and wicked member of the family, we shall continue from time to time to speed a questing arrow in the general direction of the furtive coyote.

XI

DEER HUNTING

Deer are the most beautiful animals of the woods. Their grace, poise, agility, and alertness make them a lovely and inspiring sight. To see them feed undisturbed is wonderful; such mincing steps, such dainty nibbling is a lesson in culture. With wide, lustrous eyes, mobile ears ever listening, with moist, sensitive nostrils testing every vagrant odor in the air, they are the embodiment of hypersensitive self-preservation. And yet deer are not essentially timid animals. They will venture far through curiosity, and I have seen them from the hilltop, being run by dogs, play and trifle with their pursuers. The dog, hampered by brush and going only by scent, follows implicitly the trail. The deer runs, leaps high barriers, doubles on his tracks, stops to browse at a tempting bush, even waits for the dog to catch up with him, and leads him on in a merry chase. I feel sure that unless badly cornered or confused by a number of dogs or wolves, the deer does not often develop great fear, nor is he hard put to it in these episodes. Quite likely there is an element of sport in it with him.

Why men should kill deer is a moot question, but it is a habit of the brute. For so many hundreds of years have we been at it, that we can hardly be expected to reform immediately. Undoubtedly, it is a sign of undeveloped ethnic consciousness. We are depraved animals. I must admit that there are quite a number of things men do that mark them as far below the angels, but in a way I am glad of it. The thrill and glow of nature is strong within us. The great primitive outer world is still unconquered, and there are impulses within the breast of man not yet measured, curbed and devitalized, which are the essential motives of life. Therefore, without wantonness, and without cruelty, we shall hunt as long as the arm has strength, the eye glistens, and the heart throbs.

Lead on!

To go deer hunting, the archer should seek a country unspoiled by civilization and gunpowder. It should approach as nearly as possible the pristine wilderness of our forefathers. The game should be unharried by the omnipresent and dangerous nimrod. In fact, as a matter of safety, an archer particularly should avoid those districts overrun by the gunman. The very methods employed by the bowman make him a ready target for the unerring, accidental bullet.

Never go in company with those using firearms; never carry firearms. The first spoils your hunting, and the second is unnecessary and only gives your critic a chance to say that you used a gun to kill your animal, then stuck it full of arrows to take its picture.

On our deer hunts we first decide upon the location, usually in some mountain ranch owned by a man who is willing and anxious to have us hunt on his grounds. The sporting proposition of shooting deer with a bow strikes the fancy of most men in the country. If we are unfamiliar with the district, the rancher can give us valuable information concerning the location of bucks, and this saves time. Usually he is our guide and packer, supplying the horses and equipment for a compensation, so we are welcome. Some of the intimate relations established on these expeditions are among the pleasantest features of our vacation.

Having reached the hunting grounds, we make camp. Tents are pitched, stores unpacked and arranged, beds made and all put in order for a stay of days or weeks.

Each archer has with him two or more bows, and anywhere from two to six dozen arrows. About half of these are good broad-heads and the rest are blunts or odd scraps to be shot away at birds on the wing, at marks, or some are shot in pure exhilaration across deep canyons.

As a rule, there are two or three of us in the party, and we hunt together.

Having decided what seems the best buck ground, we rise before daylight and, having eaten, strike out to reach the proposed spot before sunrise. There we spread out, approximately a bowshot apart, that is to say, two hundred yards. In parallel courses we traverse the country; one just below the ridges where one nearly always finds a game trail; one part way down, working through the wooded draws; and the third going through the timber edge where deer are likely to lurk or bed down.

In this way we cross-cut a good deal of country, and one or the other is likely to come upon or rout out a buck. With great caution we progress very quietly, searching every bit of cover, peering at every fallen log, where deer often lie, standing to scrutinize every conspicuous twig in anticipation that it may be horns. Does, of course, we see in plenty. So carefully do we approach that often we have come up within ten yards of female deer. Once Compton sneaked up on a doe nursing her fawn. He crept so close that he could have thrown his hat on them. While he watched, the mother got restless, seemed to sense danger without scenting or seeing it. She moved off slowly, pulling her teats out of the eager fawn's mouth, gave a flip to her hind legs and hopped over him, then meandered leisurely to the crest of the hill. The little fellow, unperturbed, licked his chops, ran his tongue up his nose, shook his ears, and seeing mother waiting for him, trotted away unaware of the possible danger of man. But we do not shoot does.

So we travel. Sometimes a startled deer bounds down the hillside leaving us chagrined and disappointed. Sometimes one tries this and is defeated. One evening as we returned to camp, making haste because of the rapidly falling night, we startled a deer that plunged down the steep slope before us. Instantly Compton drew to the head and shot. His arrow led the bounding animal by ten yards. Just as the deer reached cover at a distance of seventy-five yards, the arrow struck. It entered his flank, ranged forward and emerged at the point of the opposite shoulder. The deer turned and dashed into the bush. As it did so the protruding arrow shaft snapped; we descended and picked up the broken piece. Following the crashing descent of the buck down the canyon, we found him some two hundred yards below, crumpled up and dead against a madrone tree. It was a heart shot, one of the finest I ever hope to see. Compton is a master at the judgment of distance and the speed of running game.

Having worked out a piece of country by the method of sub-division, we meet at a pre-arranged rendezvous and plan another sortie.

If the sun has not risen above the peaks, we continue this method of combing the land until we know the time for bucks has passed. For this reason we work the high points first, and the lower points last, for in this way we take advantage of the slowly advancing illumination.

Sometimes, using glasses, we pick out a buck at a considerable distance, either in his solitary retreat, or with a band of deer; and we go after him. Here we figure out where he is traveling and make a detour to intercept him. This is often heartbreaking work, up hill and down dale, but all part of the game.

Young and Compton brought low a fine buck by this means on one of our recent hunts. Seeing a three-pointer a mile distant, we all advanced at a rapid pace. We reached suitable vantage ground just as the buck became aware of our presence. At eighty yards Young shot an arrow and pierced him through the chest. The deer leaped a ravine and took refuge in a clump of bay trees. We surrounded this cover and waited for his exit. Since he did not come out after due waiting, Compton cautiously invaded the wooded area, saw the wounded deer deep in thought; he finished him with a broad-head through the neck.

Not having had any large experience myself in hunting deer with firearms, the use of the bow presented no great contrast. Mr. Young has often said, however, that it gave him more pleasure to shoot at a deer and miss it with an arrow, than to kill all the deer he ever had with a gun. For my part, I did not want to kill anything with a gun. It did not seem fair; so until I took up archery, I did not care to hunt.

Therefore, the analysis of my feelings interested me considerably as we began to have experiences with the bow.

The first deer I shot at was so far off that there was no chance to hit it, but I let drive just to get the sensation. My arrow sailed harmlessly over its back. The next I shot at was within good range, but my arrow only grazed its rump. And that deer did something that I never saw before. It sagged in the middle until its belly nearly touched the ground, then it gathered its seemingly weakened legs beneath it, and galloped off in a series of bucks. We laughed immoderately over its antics; in fact, some of our adventures have been most ludicrous at times.

Once, when two of us shot at an old stag together as it raced far off down the trail, the two arrows dropped twenty yards ahead of it. Instantly the stag came to an abrupt stop, smelled first one arrow at one side of the trail, and the other on the opposite side, deliberated a moment, bolted sidewise and disappeared. What he got in his olfactory investigation must have been confusing. He smelled man; he smelled turkey feathers; and he smelled paint. What sort of animals do you think he imagined the arrows to be?

This reminds me that Ishi always said that a white man smelled like a horse, and in hunting made a noise like one, but apparently he doesn't always have horse sense.

I saw this exemplified upon one occasion. When camped in a beautiful little spot we were disturbed by the arrival of a party of some four men, five horses, and three dogs—all heavily accoutred for the chase. With our quiet Indian methods, we caused little excitement in the land, but they burst in upon us with a fury that warned all game for miles around.

The day after their arrival, alone on a trail, I heard one of this band approaching; half a mile above me his noise preceded him. Down he came over brush and stones. I stepped quietly beside a bush and waited as I would for an oncoming elephant. With gun at right shoulder arms, knapsack and canteen rattling, spiked shoes crunching, he marched past me, eyes straight ahead; walking within ten yards and never saw me. Twenty deer must have seen him where he saw one. That night this same man came straggling wearily into our midst and asked the way to his camp. He explained that he had put a piece of paper on a tree to guide him, but that he could not find the tree. We asked him what luck. He said that there were only does in the country. Perhaps he was right, because that is all they shot. We found two down in the gullies after they had gone. For a week they hunted all over the place with horses, guns, and dogs, and got no legitimate game. During this same time, beneath their very noses, we got two fine bucks. So much for the men of iron.

The first buck I ever landed with the bow thrilled me to such an extent that every detail is memorable. After a long, hard morning hunt, I was returning to camp alone. It was nearly noon; the sun beat down on the pungent dust of the trail, and all nature seemed sleepy. The air, heavy with the fragrance of the pines, hardly stirred.

I was walking wearily along thinking of food, when suddenly my outer visual fields picked up the image of a deer. I stopped. There, eighty yards away, stood a three-year-old buck, grazing under an oak. His back was toward me. I crouched and sneaked nearer. My arrow was nocked on the string. The distance I measured carefully with my eye; it was now sixty-five yards. Just then the deer raised its head. I let fly an arrow at its neck. It flew between its horns. The deer gave a started toss to its head, listened a second, then dipped its crest again to feed. I nocked another shaft. As it raised its head again I shot. This arrow flew wide of the neck, but at the right elevation. The buck now was more startled and jumped so that it stood profile to me, looking and listening. I dropped upon one knee. A little rising ground and intervening brush partially concealed me. As I drew a third arrow from my quiver its barb caught in the rawhide, and I swore a soft vicious oath to steady my nerves. Then drawing my bow carefully, lowering my aim and holding like grim death, I shot a beautifully released arrow. It sped over the tops of the dried grass seeming to skim the ground like a bird, and struck the deer full and hard in the chest. It was a welcome thud. The beast leaped, bounded off some thirty yards, staggered, drew back its head and wilted in the hind legs. I had stayed immovable as wood. Seeing him failing, I ran swiftly forward, and almost on the run at forty yards I drove a second arrow through his heart. The deer died instantly.

Conflicting emotions of compassion and exultation surged through me, and I felt weak, but I ran to my quarry, lifted his head on my knee and claimed him in the name of Robin Hood.

Looking him over, it was apparent that my second shaft had hit him in the base of the heart, emerged through the breast and only stopped in its flight by striking the foreleg. The first arrow had gone completely through the back part of the chest, severed the aorta, and flown past him. There it lay, sticking deep into the ground twenty yards beyond the spot where he stood when shot.

After the body had been cleaned and cooled in the shade of an oak, we packed it home in the twilight, an easy burden for a light heart. This is the fulfilment of the hunter's quest. It was the sweetest venison we ever tasted.

We have had little experience in trailing deer on the snow and none in the use of dogs to run them. Doubtless, the latter method under some conditions is admirable, particularly in very brushy countries.

But we have preferred the still hunt. Lying in wait at licks we have done so to study animal life and in conjunction with the Indian to learn his methods, but neither the lick nor the ambush appealed to us as sport. In fact, we have hunted deer more for meat than for trophies, and quite a number of our kills have been in a way incidental to hunting mountain lions or other predatory animals.

Once, when on a lion trail, the dogs ran down a steep trail ahead of me, and there in the creek bottom they started a fine large buck. On each side of the path the brush was very high, and up this corridor dashed the buck. There was no room for him to pass, and he came upon me with a rush. When less than twenty yards away, I hastily drew my bow and drove an arrow deep into his breast. With a lateral bound he cleared the brushy hedge and was lost to view. The dogs had been trained not to follow deer; but since they saw me shoot it, they ran in hot pursuit. I sounded my horn and brought them back, and scolded them. But fearing to lose the deer, I decided to go down to the ranch house, a couple of miles away, and borrow Jasper and his dog, Splinters. Now Splinters was some sort of a mongrel fise, an insignificant-looking little beast that had come originally from the city and presumably was hopelessly civilized. Jasper, however, had recognized in him certain latent talents and had trained him to follow wounded deer. He paid no attention to any scent except that of deer blood. In an accidental encounter with the hind foot of a horse, Splinters had lost the sight of one eye and the use of one ear; but in spite of the lopsided progression occasioned by this disability, he was infallible with wounded bucks.

So Jasper came, and Splinters trotted along at his heels. At the spot where the deer leaped off the trail, we let the dog smell a drop of blood. After a deliberate, unexcited investigation, he began to wander through the brush. Occasionally he stopped to stand on his hind legs and nose the chaparral above him, then wandered on. Just about this time I stepped on a rattlesnake, and, after a hasty change of location, directed my efforts toward dispatching the snake. By the time I had finished this worthy deed, Jasper and Splinters were lost to view; so I sat down and waited. After a quarter of an hour I heard a distant whistle.

Following Jasper's signal, I descended to the creek below me, went a short distance up a side branch, and there were all three—Jasper, Splinters, and the deer. The latter had made almost a complete circle, half a mile in extent, and dropped in the creek, not a hundred yards from his starting point.

My arrow had caused a most destructive wound in the lungs and great vessels of the chest, and it was remarkable that the animal could have gone so far. We were of the opinion that if my own dogs had not started to run him, the deer would have gone but a short distance and lain down where in a few minutes we could have found him dead.

While, after all, the object of deer hunting is to get your deer, it does seem that some of our keenest delight has been when we have missed it. So far, we have never shot one of those massive old bucks with innumerable points to his antlers; they have all been adolescent or prospective patriarchs. But several times we have almost landed the big fellow.

Out of the quiet purple shadow of the forest one evening there stepped the most stately buck I ever saw. His noble crest and carriage were superb. On a grassy hillside, some hundred and fifty yards away, he stood broadside on. With a rifle the merest tyro might have bowled him over. In fact, he looked just like the royal stag in the picture.

Two of us were together—a little underbrush shielded us. We drew our bows, loosed the arrows and off they flew. The flight of an arrow is a beautiful thing; it is grace, harmony, and perfect geometry all in one. They flew, and fell short. The deer only looked at them. We nocked again and shot. This time we dropped them just beneath his belly. He jumped forward a few paces and stopped to look at us. Slowly we reached for a third arrow, slowly nocked and drew it, and away it went, whispering in the air. One grazed his withers, the other pierced him through the loose skin of the brisket and flew past.

With an upward leap he soared away in the woods and we sent our blessing with him. His wound would heal readily, a mere scratch. We picked up our arrows and returned to camp to have bacon for supper, perfectly happy.

An arrow wound may be trivial, as was this one, or it may be surprisingly deadly, as brought out by an experience of Arthur Young. Once when stalking deer, the animal became alarmed and started to run away behind a screen of scrub oak. Young, perceiving that he was about to lose his quarry, shot at the indistinct moving body. Thinking that he had missed his shot, he searched for his arrow and found that it had plowed up the ground and buried its head deep in the earth. When he picked it up, he noted that it was strangely damp, but since he could not explain it, he dismissed the matter from his mind.

Next day, hunting over the same ground, he and Compton found the deer less than a hundred and fifty yards from this spot. It had run, fallen, bled, risen and fallen down hill, where it died of hemorrhage. Their inspection showed that the arrow had struck back of the shoulder, gone through the lungs and emerged beneath the jaw. With all this it had flown yards beyond, struck deeply in the earth, and was only a trifle damp.

Upon another occasion, while hunting cougars with a hound, I came abruptly upon a doe and a buck in a deep ravine. It was open season and we needed camp meat. Gauging my distance carefully, I shot at the buck, striking him in the flank. For the first time in my life, I heard an adult deer bleat. He gave an involuntary exclamation, whirled, but since he knew not the location or the nature of his danger, he did not run.

My hound was working higher up in the canyon, but he heard the bleat, when like a wild beast he came charging through the undergrowth and hurled himself with terrific force upon the startled deer, bearing him to the ground. There was a fierce struggle for a brief moment in which the buck wrenched himself free from the dog's hold upon his throat and with an effort lunged down the slope and eluded us. Because of the many deer trails and because the hound was unused to following deer, night fell before we could locate him.

Next day we found the dead buck, but the lions had left little meat on his bones—in fact, it seemed that a veritable den of these animals had feasted on him.

The striking picture in my mind today is the fierceness and the savage onslaught of my dog. Never did I suspect that the amiable, gentle pet of our fireside could turn into such an overpowering, indomitable killer. His assault was absolutely bloodthirsty. I've often thought how grateful I should be that such an animal was my friend and companion in the hunt and not my pursuer. How quickly the dog adjusts himself to the bow! At first he is afraid of the long stick. But he soon gets the idea and not waiting for the detonation of the gun, he accepts the hum of the bowstring and the whirr of the arrow as signals for action. Some dogs have even shown a tendency to retrieve our arrows for us, and nothing suits them better than that we go on foot, and by their sides can run with them and with our silent shafts can lay low what they bring to bay. In fact, it is a perfect balance of power—the hound with his wondrous nose, lean flanks and tireless legs; the man with his human reason, the horn, and his bow and arrow.

We who have hunted thus, trod the forest trails, climbed the lofty peaks, breathed the magic air, and viewed the endless roll of mountain ridges, blue in the distance, have been blessed by the gods.

In all, we have shot about thirty deer with the bow. The majority of these fell before the shafts of Will Compton, while Young and I have contributed in a smaller measure to the count. Despite the vague regrets we always feel at slaying so beautiful an animal, there is an exultation about bringing into camp a haunch of venison, or hanging the deer on the limb of a sheltering tree, there to cool near the icy spring. By the glow of the campfire we broil savory loin steaks, and when done eating, we sit in the gloaming and watch the stars come out. Great Orion shines in all his glory, and the Hunters' Moon rises golden and full through the skies.

Drowsy with happiness, we nestle down in our sleeping bags, resting on a bed of fragrant boughs, and dream of the eternal chase.

XII
BEAR HUNTING

Killing bears with the bow and arrow is a very old pastime, in fact, it ranks next in antiquity to killing them with a club. However, it has faded so far into the dim realms of the past that it seems almost mythical.

The bear has stood for all that is dangerous and horrible for ages. No doubt, our ancestral experiences with the cave bears of Europe stamped the dread of these mighty beasts indelibly in our hearts. The American Indians in times gone past killed them with their primitive weapons, but even they have not done it lately, so it can be considered a lost art.

The Yana's method of hunting bears has been described. Here they made an effort to shoot the beast in the open mouth. Ishi said that the blood thus choked and killed him. But after examining the bear skulls, it seems to me that a shot in the mouth is more likely to be fatal because the base of the brain is here covered with the thinnest layers of bone. Arrows can hardly penetrate the thick frontal bones of the skull, but up through the palate there would be no difficulty in entering the brain. At any rate, it is here that the Yana directed their shots. Apparently, from Ishi's description, it took quite a time to wear down and slay the animal.

All Indians seem to have had a wholesome respect for the grizzly, the mighty brother of the mountains, and they gave him the right of way.

The black bear is, of course, the same animal whether brown or cinnamon, these color variations are simply brunette, blonde and auburn complexions, the essential anatomical and habit characteristics are identical.

The American black bear at one time ranged all over the United States and Canada. He has recently become a rare inhabitant of the eastern and more thickly populated districts; yet it is astonishing to hear that even in the year of 1920 some four hundred and sixty-five bears were taken in the State of Pennsylvania.

In the western mountains he is to be met with quite frequently, but is not given to unprovoked attack, and with modern firearms an encounter with him is not fraught with great danger. He, or more properly, she will charge man with intent to kill upon certain rare occasions—when wounded, surprised, or when feeling that her young are in danger. But the bear, in company with all the other animals of the wilds, has learned to fear man since gunpowder was invented. Prior to this time, it felt the game was more equal, and seldom avoided a meeting, even courted it.

Bears are a mixture of the curious comedy traits with cunning and savage ferocity. In some of their lighter moods and pilfering habits, they add to the gayety of life.

While hunting in Wyoming one night, on coming to camp we discovered a young black bear robbing our larder. He had a ham bone in his jaws as we approached. Hastily nocking a blunt arrow on my bowstring, I let fly at sixty yards as he started to make his escape. I did not wish to kill, only admonish him. The arrow flew in a swift chiding stroke and smote him on his furry side with a dull thud. With a grunt and a bound, he dropped the bone and scampered off into the forest while the arrow rattled to the ground. His antics of surprise were most ludicrous. We sped him on his way with hilarious shouts; he never came again.

Upon a different occasion with another party, where the camp was bothered by the midnight foraging of a bear, our guide arranged to play a practical joke upon a certain "tenderfoot." Unknown to the victim, he tied a chunk of bacon to the corner of his sleeping bag with a piece of bale wire. In the middle of the night the camp was awakened by a pandemonium as the sleeping bag, man and all disappeared down the slope and landed in the creek bed below, where the determined bear, hanging on to the bacon, dragged the protesting tenderfoot. Here he abandoned his noisy burden and left the scene of excitement. No doubt, this goes down in the annals of both families as the most dramatic and stirring moment of life.

Bear stories of this sort tend to give one the idea that these beasts can be petted and made trustworthy companions. In fact, certain sentimental devotees of nature foster the sentiment that wild animals need naught but kindness and loving thoughts to become the bosom friend of man. Such sophists would find that they had made a fatal mistake if they could carry out their theories. The old feud between man and beast still exists and will exist until all wild life is exterminated or is semi-domesticated in game preserves and refuges.

Even domestic cattle allowed to run wild are extremely dangerous. Their fear of man breeds their desperate assault when cornered.

The black bear has killed and will kill men when brought to bay or wounded or even when he feels himself cornered.

Although largely vegetarian, bear also capture and devour prey. Young deer, marmots, ground squirrels, sheep, and cattle are their diet. In certain districts great damage is done to flocks by bears that have become killers. In our hunts we have come across dead sheep, slain and partially devoured by black bears. All ranchers can tell of the depredations of these animals.

In Oregon and the northern part of California, there are many men who make it their business to trap or run bears with dogs to secure their hides and to sell their meat to the city markets. It is a hardy sport and none but the most stalwart and experienced can hope to succeed at it. In the late autumn and early winter the bears are fat and in prime condition for capture.

Having graduated from ground squirrels, quail and rabbits, and having laid low the noble deer, we who shoot the bow became presumptuous and wanted to kill bear with our weapons. So, learning of a certain admirable hunter up in Humboldt County by the name of Tom Murphy, we wrote to him with our proposal. He was taken with the idea of the bow and arrow and invited us to join him in some of his winter excursions.

In November, 1918, we arrived in the little village of Blocksburg, on the outskirts of which was Murphy's ranch. In normal times, Tom cuts wood, and raises cattle and grain for the market. In the winter months he hunts bear for profit and recreation. In the spring after his planting is done he also runs coyotes with dogs and makes a good income on bounties.

We found Murphy a quiet-spoken, intelligent man of forty-five years, married, and having two daughters. I was surprised to see such a redoubtable bear-slayer so modest and kindly. We liked him immediately. It is an interesting observation that all the notable hunters that have guided us on our trips have been rather shy, soft-spoken men who neither smoked nor drank.

Arthur Young and I constituted the archery brigade. We brought with us in the line of artillery two bows and some two dozen arrows apiece. We also brought our musical instruments. Not only do we shoot, but in camp we sit by the fire at night and play sweet harmonies till bedtime. Young is a finished violinist, and he has an instrument so cut down and abbreviated that with a short violin bow he can pack it in his bed roll. Its sound is very much like that of a violin played with a mute.

My own instrument was an Italian mandolin with its body reduced to a box less than three inches square. It also is carried in a blanket roll and is known as the camp mosquito.

Young is a master at improvising second parts, double stopping, and obbligato accompaniments. So together we call all the sweet melodies out of the past and play on indefinitely by ear. In the glow of the camp-fire, out in the woods, this music has a peculiar plaintive appeal dear to our hearts.

With these charms we soon won the Murphy family and Tom was eager to see us shoot. He had heard that we shot deer, but he was rather skeptical that our arrows could do much damage to bear. So one of the first things he did after our arrival was to drag out an old dried hide and hang it on a fence in the corral and asked me to shoot an arrow through it. It was surely a test, for the old bear had been a tough customer and his hide was half an inch thick and as hard as sole leather.

But I drew up at thirty yards and let drive at the neck, the thickest portion. My arrow went through half its length and transfixed a paw that dangled behind. Tom opened his eyes and smiled. "That will do," he said, "if you can get into them that far, that's all you need. I'll take you out tomorrow morning, but I'll pack the old Winchester rifle just for the sake of the dogs."

The dogs were Tom's real asset, and his hobby. There were five of them. The two best, Baldy and Button, were Kentucky coon hounds in their prime, probably being descendants of the English fox hound with the admixture of harrier and bloodhound strains. Their breed has been in the family for thirty years. Tom took great pride in his pack, trained them to run nothing but bear and mountain lions, and never let anybody else touch them. When not hunting they are kept fastened by a sliding leash to a long heavy wire. Their diet was boiled cracked wheat and cracklings, raw apples, and bear meat. They never tasted deer meat or beef. I never saw more intelligent nor better conditioned hounds.

With the same stock he has hunted ever since he was a boy, and their lineage is more important than that of the Murphys. He has taken from ten to twenty bears every winter with these dogs for the past thirty years.

We were to stay right in Tom's house, and go by horseback to the bear grounds next morning. We had a supper which included bear steaks from a previous hunt, and doughnuts fried in bear grease, which they say is the best possible material for this culinary process, and later we greased our bows with bear grease, and our shoes with a mixture of bear fat and rosin. So we felt ready for bear.

Then we spent a delightful evening with the family before the big fireplace, played our soft music, and all turned in for an early start in the morning.

At four o'clock Tom began stirring around, building the fire and feeding the horses. An hour later we breakfasted and were ready to start. Light snow had fallen in the hills and the air was chill; the moon was sinking in the valley mist. These early morning hours in the country are strange to us who live so far from nature.

We mount and are off. As we go the horses see the trail that we cannot discern, vague forms slip past, a skunk steals off before us, an owl flaps noiselessly past, overhanging brush sweeps our faces, the dogs leashed in couples trot ahead of us like spectres in procession.

Thus we journey for nearly ten miles in the darkness, going up out of the valley, on to the foothills, through Windy Gap, past Sheep Corral, over the divide, heading toward the Little Van Duzen River.

All the while the dogs amble along, sniffing here and there at obscure scents, now loitering to investigate a moment, now standing and looking off into the dark. Tom knows by their actions what they think. "That's a coyote's trail," he says, "they've just crossed a deer scent, but they won't pay much attention to that." Their demeanor is self-possessed and un-excited.

At last, just before dawn, we arrive on a pine-covered hillside and the dogs become more eager. This is the bear country. They cross the canyon here to get to the forest of young oak trees, beyond where the autumn crop of acorns lies ready to fatten them for their long winter sleep.

Here is a bear tree, a small pine or fir, stripped of limbs and bark, against which countless bears have scratched themselves.

Tom looses the dogs and sends them ranging to pick up a scent. They take to it with eagerness, and soon we hear the boom of the hounds on a cold track. Tom gets interested, but shakes his head. Last night's snowfall and later drizzle have spoiled the ground for good tracking. We dismount, tie our horses and follow the general direction of the pack. They must be kept within earshot so that when they strike a hot track we can keep up with them. If there is much wind and the forest noises are loud, Tom will not run his dogs for fear of losing them. Once on the trail of a bear, they never quit, but will leave the country rather than give him up.

Expectation, stimulated by the distant baying of the running hounds, the cold gray shadows of the woods, and the knowledge that any moment a bear may come crashing through the undergrowth right where we stand, tends to hold one in a state of exquisite suspense—not fear, just chilly suspense. In fact, I was rather glad to see the sun rise.

But nothing came of this hunt. We worked over the creek bottom below, rode over adjacent hills and canyons, struck cold trails here and there to assure us that bear really existed, then at about ten o'clock Murphy decided that weather conditions of the night before, combined with the dissipating effect of sunshine and the lateness of the hour, all dictated that we had best give up the game for that day.

So back we rode, the dogs a trifle footsore, for they had covered many a mile in their ranging. Tom had shoes for them to wear when they are very lame at the first of the season. Later on, their feet become tough and need no protection. So we arrived back at the ranch empty-handed.

Next day we rested, and rain fell.

The day following we again tried a hunt and again failed to strike a hot track. Tom was perplexed, for it was a rare thing for him to return home without a bear. He rather suspected that the bows were a "jinx" and brought bad luck. So again we rested the dogs and waited for a change of fortune.

The time between hunts Young and I spent shooting rabbits. Once when down on the stream bank looking for trout, Young saw a female duck diving beneath the surface of the water. As it rose he shot it with an arrow and nocking a second shaft, he prepared to deliver a finishing blow if necessary, when up the stream he heard the whirring wings of a flying duck; instantly he drew his bow, glanced to the left, and shot at the rapidly approaching male. Pinioned through the wings, it dropped near the first victim and he gathered the two as a tidbit for supper.

These things do happen between our larger adventures, and delight us greatly.

The evenings we spent before the fire, played music, and I performed sleights of hand, much to the wonderment of the rural audience that gathered to see the strangers who expected to kill bears with bows and arrows. After numerous coin tricks, card passes, mysterious disappearances, productions of wearing apparel and cabbages from a hat, and many other incredible feats of prestidigitation, they were almost ready to believe we might slay bears with our bows.

Tom's dogs having recovered from our previous unsuccessful trips, we started again one crisp frosty morning with the stars all aglitter overhead. This time we were sure of good luck. Mrs. Murphy was positive we would bring home a bear; she felt it in her bones.

It is cold riding this time in the morning, but it is beautiful. The snow-laden limbs of the firs drop their loads upon us as we pass, the twigs are whip-like in their recoil as they strike our legs; the horses pick their way with surefooted precision, and we wonder what adventures wait for us in the silent gloom.

This time we rode far. If bears were to be had any place, they could be found in Panther Canyon, below Mt. Lassie.

By sunrise we reached the ridge back of the desired spot where we tied our horses preparatory to climbing up the gulch. The dogs were made ready; there were only three of them this time: Button, Baldy, and old Buck, the shepherd dog. Immediately they struck a cold trail and danced around in a circle, baying with long deep bell tones, pleading to be released. My breath quivers at the memory of them. Murphy unclasped the chains that linked them together and they scampered up the precipitous ravine before us. As they passed, Tom pointed out bear tracks, the first we had seen.

In less than ten minutes the full-throated bay of the hounds told us that they had struck a hot track and routed the bear from his temporary den.

That was the signal for speed, and we began a desperate race up the side of the mountain. Nothing but perfect physical health can stand such a strain. One who is not in athletic training will either fail completely in the test or do his heart irreparable damage.

But we were fit; we had trained for the part. Stripped for action, we were dressed in hunting breeches, light high-topped shoes spiked on the soles, in light cotton shirts, and carried only our bows, quivers of arrows, and hunting knives. Tom was a seasoned mountain climber, born on the crags, and had knees like a goat. So we ran. Up the side and over the crest we sped. The bay of the hounds pealed out with every bound ahead of us. As we crossed the ridge, we heard them down the canyon below us, the crashing of the bear and the cry of the dogs thrilled us with a very old and a very strong flood of emotions. Panting and flushed with effort we rushed onward; legs, legs, and more air, 'twas all we wanted. Tom is tough and used to altitudes, Young is stronger and more youthful than I am, and besides a flapping quiver, an unwieldy bow, my camera banged me unmercifully on the back. Still I kept up very well, and my early sprinting on the cinder track came to my aid. We stuck together, but just as I had about decided that running was a physical impossibility, Tom shouted, "He is treed." That was a welcome word. We slackened our pace, knowing that the dogs would hold him till we arrived, and we needed our breath for the next act. So on a trot we came over a rise of ground and saw, away up on the limb of a tall straight fir tree, a bear that looked very formidable and large. The golden rays of the rising sun were shining through his fur.

That was the first bear I had ever seen in the open, first wild bear, first bear with no iron bars between him and me. I felt peculiar.

The dogs were gathered beneath the tree keeping up a chorus of yelps and assaulting its base as if to tear it to pieces. The bear apparently had no intention of coming down.

Tom had instructed us fully what to do; so we now helped him catch his dogs and tie them with a rope which he held. He did this because he knew that if we wounded the bear and he descended there was going to be a fight, and he didn't want to lose his valuable dogs in an experiment. He had his gun to take care of himself, and Young and I were supposed to stand our share of the adventure as best we could.

Keen with anticipation of unexpected surprises; wondering, yet willing to take a chance, we prepared to shoot our first bear. We stationed ourselves some thirty yards from the base of the tree. The bear was about seventy-five feet up in the air, facing us, looking down and exposing his chest.

We drew our arrows together and a second later released as one man. Away flew the two shafts, side by side, and struck the beast in the breast, not six inches apart. Like a flash, they melted into his body and disappeared forever. He whirled, turned backward, and began sliding down the tree.

Ripping and tearing the trunk, he descended almost as if falling, a shower of bark preceding him like a cartload of shingles. Tom shouted, "You missed him, run up close and shoot him again!" From his side of the tree he couldn't see that our arrows had hit and gone through, also he was used to seeing bear drop when he hit them with a bullet.

But we were a little diffident about running up close to a wounded bear, for Tom had told us it would fight when it got down. Nevertheless, we nocked an arrow again, and just as he reached the ground we were close by to receive him. We delivered two glancing blows on his rapidly falling body. When he landed, however, he selected the lower side of the tree, away from us, and bounded off down the canyon. We protested that we had hit him and begged Tom to turn his dogs loose. After a moment's deliberation, Tom let old Buck go and off he tore in hot pursuit. The shepherd was a wily old cattle dog and would keep out of harm.

Soon we heard him barking and Murphy exclaimed incredulously, "He's treed again!" Button and Baldy were unleashed and once more we started our cross-country running. Through maple thickets, over rocky sides, down the wooded canyon we galloped. Much sooner than we expected, we came to our bear. Hard pressed, he had climbed a small oak and crouched out on a swaying limb. We could see that he was heaving badly, and was a very sick animal. His gaze was fixed on the howling dogs. Young and I ran in close and shot boldly at his swaying body. Our arrows slipped through him like magic. One was arrested in its course as it buried itself in his shoulder. Savagely he snapped it in two with his teeth, when another driven by Young with terrific force struck him above the eye. He weakened his hold, slipped backward, dropped from the bending limb and rolled over and over down the ravine. The dogs were on him in a rush, and wooled him with a vengeance. But he was dead by the time he reached the creek bottom. We clambered down, looked him over with awe, then Young and I shook hands across the body of our first bear. We took his picture.

Tom opened up the chest and abdominal cavity, explored the wounds and was full of exclamations of surprise at the damage done by our arrows. He agreed that our animal was mortally wounded with our first two shots, and had we let him alone there would have been no necessity for more arrows. But this being our very first bear, we had overdone the killing.

So he gave the liver and lungs to the waiting hounds as a reward for their efforts, and cleaned the carcass for carrying. We found the stomach full of acorn mush, just as clean and sweet as a mess of cornmeal.

Murphy left us to pack the bear up on the pine flat above, while he went around three or four miles to get the horses. After a strenuous half hour, we got our bear up the steep bank and rested on the flat. Here we ate our pocket lunch.

As we sat there quietly eating, we heard a rustle in the woods below us, and looking up, saw another good-sized black bear about forty yards off. I had one arrow left in my quiver, Young only two broken shafts, the rest we had lost in our final scramble. So we passed no insulting remarks to the bear below, who suddenly finding our presence, vanished in the forest. We had had enough bear for one day, anyhow.

Tom came with the horses, and loaded our trophy on one. Ordinarily a horse is greatly frightened at bears, and difficult to manage, but these were long ago accustomed to the business. It interested us to see the method of tying the carcass securely on a common saddle. By placing a clove hitch on the wrists and ankles and cinching these beneath the horse's belly with a sling rope through the bear's crotch and around its neck, the body was held suspended across the saddle and rode easily without shifting until we reached home.

Adult black bear range in weight from one hundred to five hundred pounds. Ours, although he had looked very formidable up the tree, was really not a very large animal and not fully grown. After cleaning, it tipped the scales at a little below two hundred pounds. But it was large enough for our purposes, and we couldn't wait for it to grow any heavier. It was no fault of ours that it was only some three or four years old. We felt that even had it been one of those huge old boys, we would have conquered him just the same. In fact, we had begun to count ourselves among the intrepid bear slayers of the world. So we returned to the ranch in triumph.

Next day we took our departure from Blocksburg and bade the Murphys an affectionate farewell. The bear we carried with us wrapped in canvas to distribute in luscious steaks to our friends in the city. The beautiful silky pelt now rests on the parlor floor of Young's home with a ferocious wide open mouth waiting to scare little children, or trip up the unwary visitor.

Since this, our maiden bear, we have had various other encounters with bruin. Once while hunting mountain lions, we came upon the body of an angora goat recently killed by a bear. The ground was covered with his ungainly footprints. We set the dogs on the scent and off they went, booming in hot pursuit. Running like wild Indians, Young and I followed by ear, bows ready strung and quivers held tightly to our sides. In less than ten minutes, we burst into a little open glade in the forest and saw up in a large madrone tree, a good-sized cinnamon bear fretfully eyeing the dogs below.

We had lost our apprehension concerning the outcome of an encounter with bears, so we coolly prepared to settle his fate. In fact, we even discussed the problem whether or not we should kill him. We were not after bears, but lions. This fellow, however, was a rogue, a killer of sheep and goats. He had repeatedly thrown our dogs off the track with his pungent scent and we were strictly within our hunting rights if we wanted him. We therefore drew our broadheads to the barb and drove two wicked shafts deep into his front. As if knocked backwards, the bear reared and threw himself down the slanting tree trunk. As he reached the ground, one of our dogs seized him by the hind leg and the two went flying past us within a couple of yards, the dog hanging on like grim death. Furiously, the other dogs followed and we leaped to the chase.

This time the course of the bear was marked by a swath of broken brush. It dashed headlong through the forest regardless of obstruction. Small trees in his way meant nothing to him; he ran over them, or if old and brittle, smashed them down. Into the densest portion of the woods he made his way. Not more than three hundred yards from the spot he started, he treed again. In an almost impenetrable thicket of small cedars, the dogs sent up their chorus of barks. I dashed in, fighting my way free from restraining limbs, the bow and quiver holding me again and again. Young got stuck and fell behind, so that I came alone upon our bear at bay. He had mounted but a short distance up a mighty oak and hung by his claws to the bark. I had run beneath him before seeing his position. Instantly I recognized the danger of the situation and backed off, away from the tree, at the same time nocking an arrow on the string. I glanced about for Young, but he was detained, so I drew the head and discharged my arrow right into the heart region of our beast, where it buried its point. Loosening his hold, the bear fell backward from the tree and landed on the nape of his neck. He was weak with mortal wounds, and even had he wanted to charge me, the combat could not have progressed far. But instantly the dogs were on him. Seizing him by the front and back legs, they dragged him around a small tree, holding him firmly in spite of his struggles, while he bawled like a lost calf. The din was terrific; snarling, snapping dogs, the crashing underbrush, and the bellowing of bear made the world hideous. It seemed that the pain of our arrows was nothing to him compared to his fear of the dogs, and when he felt himself helpless in their power, his morale was completely shattered.

It was soon over; hardly a minute elapsed before his resistless form lay still, and even the dogs knew he was dead. Poor Young arrived at this moment, having just extricated himself from the brush.

We skinned the pelt to make quivers, took his claws for decorations, and cut some sweet bear steaks from his hams; the rest we gave to the pack.

It seems a very proper thing that the service of the dogs should always be recognized promptly, that they be given their share of the spoils and that they be praised for their courage and fidelity. This makes them better hunters. Stupid men who drive off their dogs from the quarry, defer their rewards, and grudge them praise, kill the spirit of the chase within them and spoil them for work.

Hounds have the finest hunting spirit of any animal. The team work of the wolf and their intelligent use of strategy is one of the most striking evidences of community interests in animal life.

The fellowship between us and our dogs is a most satisfactory relation. Since prehistoric times, the hunter has taken advantage of the comradeship and on it rests the mutual dependence and trust of the two.

Altogether, bringing bears to bay is among the most thrilling experiences of life. It is a primitive sport and as such it stirs up in the human breast the primordial emotions of men. The sense of danger, the bodily exhaustion, the ancestral blood lust, the harkening bay of the hounds, the awe of deep-shadowed forests, and the return to an almost hand-to-claw contest with the beast, call upon a latent manhood that is fast disappearing in the process of civilization.

I hope there always will be bears to hunt and youthful adventurers to chase them.

XIII

MOUNTAIN LIONS

The cougar, panther, or mountain lion is our largest representative of the cat family. Early settlers in the Eastern States record the existence of this treacherous beast in their conquest of the forests. The cry of the "painter," as he was called, rang through the dark woods and caused many hearts to quaver and little children to run to mother's side. Once in a while stories came of human beings having met their doom at the swift stealthy leap of this dreaded beast. He was bolder then than now. Today he is not less courageous, but more cautious. He has learned the increased power of man's weapons.

Our Indians knew that he would strike, as they struck, without warning and at an advantage. It is a matter of tradition among frontiersmen that he has upon rare occasions attacked and killed bears. Even today he will attack man if provoked by hunger, and can do so with some assurance of success, the statements of certain naturalists to the contrary notwithstanding.

John Capen Adams, in his adventures, describes such an episode. The lion in this instance sprang upon a companion, seized him by the back of the neck, and bore him to the ground. He was only saved from death by a thick buckskin collar to his coat and the ready assistance of Adams who heard the cry for help.

I know of an instance where a California lion leaped upon some bathing children and attempted to kill them, but was driven off by the heroic efforts of a young woman school teacher, who in turn died of her wounds.

Those of us who have roamed the wilds of the western country have had varying experiences with this animal, while others have lived their lives in districts undoubtedly infested with cougars and have never seen one, although nearly every mountain rancher has heard that hair-raising, almost human scream echo down the canyon. It is like the wail of a woman in pain. Penetrating and quavering, it rings out on the night gloom, and brings to the human what it must, in a similar way, bring to the lesser animals a sense of impending attack, a death warning. It is part of the system of the predatory beast that he uses fear to weaken the powers of his prey before he assaults it. Animal psychology is essentially utilitarian. Cowering, trembling, muscularly relaxed, on the verge of emotional shock, we are easier to overcome.

The cougar lives principally on deer. His kill averages more than one a week, and often we may find evidence that this murderer has wantonly slain two or three deer in a single night's expedition.

It is not his habit to lie in wait on the limb of a tree, though he often sleeps there; but he makes a stealthy approach on the unsuspecting victim, then, with a series of stupendous bounds, he throws himself upon the deer, and by his momentum bears it to the ground.

Here, while he holds on with teeth and forelegs, he rips open the flank with his hind claws and immediately plunges his head into the open abdomen, where he tears the great blood vessels with his teeth and drinks its life blood.

These are facts learned from lion hunters whose observations are accurate and reliable. A lion can jump a distance greater than twenty-four feet, and has been seen to ascend at a single leap a cliff of rock eighteen feet high.

Their weight runs from one hundred to two hundred pounds, and the length from six to nine feet. The skin will stretch farther than this, but we count only the carcass from the tip of the nose to the tip of the extended tail. The speed of a lion for a short distance is greater than that of a greyhound, less than five seconds to the hundred yards.

Some observers contend that the lion never gives that blood-curdling cry assigned to him. They say he is silent, and that this classic scream is made by a lynx in the mating period. However, popular experience to the contrary seems to be too strong and counterbalances this iconoclastic opinion.

For many years, off and on, we have hunted lions, but sad to say, we have done more hunting than finding. They are a very wary creature. Practically, one never sees them unless hunting with dogs; they may be in the brush within thirty yards, but the human eye will fail to discern them.

Our camps have been robbed by lions, our horses killed by them, cattle and sheep ruthlessly murdered; lion tracks have been all about, and yet unless trapped or treed by dogs, we have never met.

Camping at the base of Pico Blanco, in Monterey County, several years ago, a lion was seen to bound across the road and follow a small band of deer. At this very spot a few seasons before one leaped upon an old mare with foal and broke her neck as she crashed through the fence and rolled down the hill. Three years later I rode the young horse. As we passed the tree from which it is thought the lion sprang, where the broken fence was still unmended, my colt jumped and reared, the memory of his fright was still vivid in his mind. Up the trail a half mile beyond we saw other fresh lion tracks. At night we camped on the ridge with our dogs in hope that our feline friend would come again.

It was too late to hunt that evening, so we turned in. Nothing happened save that in the middle of the night I was roused by the whine of our dogs, and looking up in the face of the pale moon, I saw two deer go bounding past, silhouetted like graceful phantoms across the silvered sky. They swept across the lunar disc and melted into blackness over the dark horizon.

No sound followed them, and having appeased the fretful hounds, we returned to sleep. In the morning, up the trail, there were his tracks; too wise to cross the human scent, and knowing that there are more deer in the brush, he had turned upon his course and let his quarry slip.

Because of the heat and the inferior tracking capacity of our dogs, we never got this panther. A lion dog is a specialist and must be so trained that no other track will divert him from his quest. These dogs were willing, but erratic.

The best dogs for this work are mongrels. By far the finest lion dog I ever saw was a cross between a shepherd and an airedale. He had the intelligence of the former and the courage of the latter. The airedale himself is not a good trailer, he is too temperamental. He will start on a lion track, jump off and chase a deer and wind up by digging out a ground squirrel. After a good hound finds a lion, the airedale will tackle him.

We once started an airedale on a lion track, followed him at a fiendish pace, dashed down the side of a mountain, and found that he had an angora goat up a tree.

This cougar on Pico Blanco still roams the forests, so far as I know, and many with him. Once we saw him across a canyon. He appeared as a tawny slow-moving body as large as a deer but low to the earth and trailing a listless tail, while his head slowly swung from side to side. He seemed to be looking for something on the ground. For the space of a hundred yards we watched him traverse an open side hill, deep in ferns and brakes. Seeing him thus was little satisfaction to us, for we had lost our dogs. Ferguson and I were returning from one of our unsuccessful expeditions.

We started with two saddle horses, a pack animal, and five good lion dogs. On the trail to the Ventana Mountains we came across lion tracks and followed them for a day, then lost them; but we knew that a large male and young female were ranging over the country. Their circuit extended over a radius of ten miles; they are great travelers.

The track of a lion is characteristic. The general contour is round, from three to four inches in diameter. There are four toe prints arranged in a semicircle which show no claw marks. But the ball of the foot is the unmistakable feature. It consists of three distinct eminences or pads which lie parallel, antero-posteriorly, and appear in the track as if you had pressed the terminal phalanges of your fingers side by side in the dust. These marks are nearly equal in length and absolutely identify the big cat.

On the morning of the second day of our trailing this lion, our pack was working down in the thick brush below the crest of Rattlesnake Ridge, when suddenly they raised a chorus of yelps. There was a rush of bodies in the chamise brush, and the chase was on at a furious pace. We rode up to an observation point and saw the dogs speeding down the canyon side, close on the heels of a yellow leaping demon. They switched from side to side, as cat and dog races have been carried on since time immemorial.

The undergrowth was so dense we could not follow, so we sat our horses and waited for them to tree. But further and further they descended. They crossed the bottom, mounted a cliff on the opposite side, came scrambling down from this and plunged into the bed of the stream, where their voices were lost to hearing.

We rode around to a spur of the hill that dipped into the brush and overhung the canyon. From this we heard occasional barks away down at least a mile below us. It was a difficult situation. Nothing but a bluejay could possibly get down to the creek below. I never saw such a jungle! So we waited for the indications that the lion was treed, but all became silent.

Evening approached, we ate our supper and then sat on the hill above, sounding our horns. Their vibrant echoes rang from mountain to mountain and returned to us clear and sweet.

Way down below us, where a purple haze hung over the deep ravine, we faintly heard the answering hounds. In their voices we caught the dog's response to his master and friend. It said, "We have him. Come! Come!" We blew the horns again. The elf-land notes returned again and again, and with them came the call of the faithful hound, "We are here. Come! Come!"

Now, there was a pitiful plight. No sane man would venture down such a chasm, impenetrable with thorns, and night descending. So we built a beacon fire and waited for dawn. All during the long dark hours we heard the distant appeal of the hounds, and we slept little.

At the first rays of dawn we took a hasty meal, fed our horses, and stripping ourselves of every unnecessary accoutrement, we prepared to descend the canyon. Our bows and quivers we left behind because it would have been impossible to drag them through the jungle. Ferguson carried only his Colt pistol; I took my hunting knife.

Having surveyed the topography carefully, we attacked the problem at its most available angle and slid from view. We literally dived beneath the brush. For more than two hours we wormed our way down the face of the mountain, crawling like moles at the base of the overhanging thickets of poison oak, wild lilac, chamise, sage, manzanita, hazel and buckthorn. At last we reached the depth of the canyon and, finding a little water, we bathed our sweat-grimed faces and cooled off.

No sound of the dogs was heard, but pressing forward we followed the boulder-strewn bottom of the creek for a mile or more, almost despairing of ever finding them, when suddenly we came upon a strange sight. There was the pack in a circle about a big reclining oak. They were voiceless and utterly exhausted, but sat watching a huge lion crouched on a great overhanging limb of the tree. The moment we appeared they raised a feeble, hoarse yelp of delight. The panther turned his head, saw us, sprang from the tree with a prodigious bound, landed on the side hill, tore down the canyon, and leaped over a precipice below.

The dogs, heartened by our presence, with instant accord charged after the lion. When they came to the precipitous drop in the bed of the stream, they whined a second, ran back and forth, then mounted the lateral wall, circled sidewise and, by a detour, gained the ground below. We ran and looked over. The drop was at least thirty feet. The cat had taken it without hesitation, but we were absolutely stalled. Even if we had cared to take the risk of the descent, we saw so many similar drops beyond that the situation was hopeless. The dogs having lost their voices, we were at a great disadvantage. So we returned to the tree to rest and meditate.

There we saw the evidence of the long vigil of the night. All about its base were little nests, where the tired dogs had bedded down and kept their weary watch. Their incessant barking had served to keep the cougar treed, but it cost them a temporary loss of voice. Poor devils, they had our admiration and sympathy.

At noon, hearing nothing from the hounds, we decided to return to camp. If coming down was hard, going up was herculean. We crawled on hands and knees, dragged ourselves by projecting roots, panted, rested, and worked again. After a three-hours' struggle we came out upon a rough ledge of granite, a mile below the spot at which we aimed, but near enough to the top to permit us, after a little more brush fighting, to gain our camp and lie down, too fatigued to eat.

For another day we remained at this place, hoping that the dogs would return, but in vain. At last we decided to pack up and go around a ten-mile detour and work up the outlet of the canyon. We left a mess of food in several piles for the dogs should they return, and knew they could follow our horses' tracks if they came to camp.

But our detour was futile. We lost all signs of our pack and returned to our headquarters to await results.

It was on this homeward journey that we saw the lion of Pico Blanco, and had to let him slip.

Ten days later, two weak, emaciated hounds came into camp, an old veteran and a young dog that trailed after him as if tied with a rope. He had followed him to save his life, and for days after he could not be separated without whining with fear.

We fed them carefully and nursed them back to health. But these were all of the five to appear. Old Belle, the greatest fighter of them all, was gone. She must have met her death at the claws of the cougar, for nothing else could keep her. This ended that particular lion hunt.

In our travels over California in search for cougars, we have picked up more tales than trails of the big cats.

Just before one of my visits to Gorda, on the Monterey Coast, a panther visited the Mansfield ranch in broad daylight. Jasper being up on the mountainside after deer, his wife, left at home with the two little children, noticed a very large lion out in the pasture back of the house. It wandered among the cattle in a most unconcerned manner and did not even cause a stir. While it did not approach any of the cows very closely, they seemed to be not in the least alarmed. For half an hour or more it stayed in the neighborhood of the house, where Mrs. Mansfield locked herself in and waited for her husband's return. It was not until evening, and too late to track the beast, that Jasper came home. So no capture was made.

Some time before this, one of the hired hands on the ranch was going to his cabin in the dusk; and swinging his hand idly to catch the tops of tall grass by the side of the path, he suddenly touched something warm and soft. Instantly he grasped a handful of the substance. At the same moment some sort of an animal bounded off in the dark. Holding fast to the material in his hand, he ran back to the farmhouse and found his fist full of lion hair. To say that he was startled, puts it very mildly. Apparently one of these beasts had been crouched on a log by the side of his path, waiting for something to turn up. The hired man took a lantern home with him after that.

At another ranch on the Big Sur River, one of the little boys called to his mother that there was a funny sort of a "big dog" out in the pasture. His mother paid no attention to it, but a diminutive pet black and tan started an assault on the animal in question. The lion and the dog disappeared in the brush. Presently the canine barking ceased and the small boy wondered what had become of his valiant companion. In a few minutes he heard a plaintive whine up in a near-by tree, and running to its base he found that the panther had seized his pet by the nape of the neck and climbed a tall fir with him. The boy ran for his father, working in the fields, who, bringing his rifle, dispatched the panther. As it fell from the tree, the little dog clung to the upper limbs, and stayed at the top. Nothing they could do would coax him down. The fir was one difficult to climb, so to save time the man took an ax and felled the tree, which, falling gently against another, precipitated the canine hero to the ground without harm. Later I had the pleasure of shaking his paw and congratulating him on his bravery.

After many futile attempts, at last our opportunity to get a *Felis Concolor* arrived. We received word from a certain ranger station in Tuolumne County that a mountain lion was killing sheep and deer in the immediate vicinity, and having the promise of a well trained pack, Arthur Young and I gathered our archery tackle and started from San Francisco at night in an automobile. We traveled until the small hours of the morning, then lay down on the side of the road to take a short sleep; and rising at the first gray of dawn, sped on our way.

We reached the Sierras by sun-up and began to climb. At noon we met our guide above Italian Bar, and prepared for an evening hunt. This, however, was as unsatisfactory as evening hunts usually are.

A morning expedition the next day only brought out the fact that our lion had left the country. News of his activities twelve miles further up the mountains having been obtained, we gathered our bows, arrows, and dogs and departed for this region. Here we found a bloody record of his work. More than two hundred goats had been killed by the big cat in the past year. In fact, the rancher thought that several panthers were at work. Goats were taken from beneath the shepherd's nose, and as he turned in one direction, another goat would be killed behind him. It seemed impossible to apprehend the villain; their dogs were useless.

Equipped for rough camping, we soon planned our morning excursion and bedded down for rest.

At 3 o'clock we waked, ate a meager breakfast, and hit the trail up the mountain. We knew the general range of our cougar. It is necessary in all his tracking to get in the field while the dew is on the ground and before the sun dissipates it, also before the goats obliterate the tracks.

Arrived at the crest of the ridge, we struck a well-defined goat trail, and soon the fresh tracks of a lion were discovered. Our dogs took up the scent at once and we began to travel at a rapid pace.

Here again, one must have a good pair of legs. If automobiles, elevators, and general laziness have not ruined your powers of locomotion, you may follow the dogs; otherwise, you had best stay at home.

At first we walk, then we trot, and when with a leap the hounds start in full cry, we race. Regardless of five thousand feet of altitude, regardless of brush, rocks, and dizzy cliffs, we follow at a breakneck pace. I don't know where our breath comes from in these trials. We just have to run; in fact, we have planned to run on our hands when our legs play out. With pounding hearts we surge ahead. "Keep the dogs within hearing!" "It can't last long!" But this time we come to a sudden halt on a rocky slide. We've lost the scent. The dogs circle and backtrack and work with feverish haste. The sun has risen, and up the mountain side comes a band of goats led by a single shepherd dog—no man in sight. We shout to the dog to steer his rabble away, but on they come, and obliterate our trail with a thousand hoofprints and a cloud of dust.

The sun then comes out, and our day is done. No felis this time.

So we scout the country for information to be used later, and return to camp to drown our sorrow in food.

This was my first knowledge that a dog could be placed in charge of a flock of sheep or goats. It seems that these little sheep dogs, not even collies, but some shaggy little plebeians, are given full charge of the band. They lead them out to pasture, guard them, and keep them together during the day and bring them home at night. They will, when properly instructed, take a band of goats out for a week on a long route, and bring them all safely home again. At least, they used to do this until the lion appeared on the scene.

That evening we asked the rancher to lock his goats in the corral till noon.

Next morning we rose again in time to see the morning star glitter with undimmed glory. Up the trail we mounted, the dogs eager for the chase. An old owl in a hollow tree asked us again and again who we were; all else was silent in the woods.

Saving our strength, we arrived quietly on the upper ridges and waited for the dawn. Way down below us in the canyon we could smell the faint incense of our camp-fire. The morning breeze was just beginning to breathe in the trees. The birds awoke with little whispered confidences, small twitterings and chirps. A faint lavender tint melted the stars in the eastern sky. Shadows crept beneath the trees, and we knew it was time to start.

Just as the light defined the margins of the trail, we picked up in the grayness the track of a lion. Strange to say, the dogs had not smelled it, but when we pointed to the footprint in the dust, which was apparently none too fresh, they took up the work of tracking. It is astonishing to see how a dog can tell which way a track leads. If in doubt, he runs quickly back and forth on the scent, and thus gauges the way the animal has progressed. A mediocre dog cannot do this, but we had dogs with college educations.

Traveling carefully and at a moderate pace, we came to an open knoll in the forest. Here in the ferns our pack circled about us as if the cat had been doing a circus stunt, and they seemed confused. Later on we found that our feline friend had been experimenting with a porcupine and learned another lesson in natural history.

Suddenly the leader sniffed at a fallen tree where, doubtless, the cat had perched, then with a ringing bay, the hound clamped his tail close to his rump and left in a streak of yellow light. The rest of the pack leaped into full cry.

We were off on a hot track. Oh, for the wings of a bird! Trained as Young and I were to desperate running, this game taxed us to the utmost. First we climbed the knoll, deep in ferns and mountain misery, then we dashed over the crest, tore through manzanita brush, thickets of young cedar and buckthorn, over ledges of lava rock, down deep declivities, among giant oaks, cedars, and pines. As we ran we grasped our ready strung bows in one hand and the flapping quivers in the other.

You would not think that at this time we could take note of the fragrant shrubs and pine needles beneath our feet, but I smelled them as we passed in flight, and they revived me to renewed energy. On we rushed, only to lose the sound of the dogs. Then we listened and caught it down the hill below us. Again we hurdled barriers of brush, took long sliding leaps down the treacherous shale and ran breathless to the shade of a great oak.

There above our heads was the lion. Oh, the beauty of that beast!

Heaving and giddy with exertion, we saw a wonderful sight, a great tawny, buff-colored body crouched on a limb, grace and power in every outline. A huge, soft cylindrical tail swung slowly back and forth.

Luminous eyes gazed at us in utmost calm, a cold calculating calm. He watched and waited our next move, waited with his great muscles tense for action.

We retreated, not only to get out of his reach, but to gain a better shooting position. As we did this, he gave a lithe leap to a higher limb and shielded himself as best he could behind the boughs of the tree.

From our position, his chest and throat were visible through a triangular space in the branches, not more than a foot across. We must shoot through this. His attitude was so huddled that his head hung over his shoulder.

Young and I caught our breath, drew our arrows from their quivers, nocked them, and set ourselves in the archer's "stable stand." We drew together and, at a mutual thought, shot together. Because of our unsteady condition the arrows flew a trifle wild. Mine buried itself in the lion's shoulder. Young's hit him in the nose.

He reared and struck at this latter shaft, then, not dislodging it, began swaying back and forth while with both front paws he fought the arrow.

While he thrashed about thus in the tree top, we nocked two more arrows and shot. We both missed the brute. Young's flew off into the next state, and if you ever go up into Tuolumne County, you will find mine buried deep in the heart of an oak.

Just as we nocked a third arrow, he freed himself from the offending shaft in his muzzle, raised his fore-paws upon a limb and prepared to leap. In that movement he bared the white hair of his throat and chest, and like a flash, two keen arrows were driven through his heart area.

As they struck and disappeared from sight, he leaped. Like a flying squirrel, he soared over our heads. Full seventy-five feet he cleared in one mighty outward, downward bound. I saw his body glint across the rising sun, swoop in a wonderful curve and land in a sheltering bush.

The dogs threw themselves upon him. There was a medley of sounds, a fierce, but brief fight, and all was over. We grabbed him by the tail and dragged him forth—dead. The ringleader of our pack, trembling with excitement, effort, and fighting frenzy, drove all the other dogs away and took possession of the body. No one but a man, his master, might touch it.

Our lion was a young male, six feet eight inches from tip to tip, and weighing a little over one hundred and twenty pounds. Later, as we skinned him, we found his paws full of porcupine quills, speaking loudly of his recent experience. The stomach was empty; the chest was full of blood from our arrows.

He was as easy to kill as a deer. We packed him back to camp and added his photograph to our rogues' gallery.

There was no further goat killing on that Sierra ranch.

This was our first lion, and for me so far, my only one. Arthur Young, however, has been fortunate enough to land two cougars by himself on another hunting trip.

Captain C. H. Styles, a recent addition to the ranks of field archers, while on an expedition to cut yew staves in Humboldt County, California, started a mountain lion, ran him to bay with hounds, and killed him with one arrow in the chest. We shall undoubtedly hear more of the captain later on.

But so long as we can draw a bowstring and our legs hold out, and there is an intelligent dog to be had, it will not be the last lion on our list. Wherever there are deer, there will be found panthers, and it is our business to help reduce their number in the game fields to maintain the balance of power.

XIV

GRIZZLY BEAR

The very idea of shooting grizzly bears with the bow and arrow strikes most people as so absurd that they laugh at the mention of it. The mental picture of the puny little archery implements of their childhood opposed to that of the largest and most fearsome beast of the Western world, produces merriment and incredulity.

Because it seemed so impossible, I presume, this added to our desire to accomplish it.

Ever since we began hunting with the bow, we had talked of shooting grizzlies. We thought of an Alaskan trip as a remotely attainable adventure, and planned murderous arrows of various ingenious spring devices to increase their cutting qualities. We estimated the power of formidable bows necessary to pierce the hides of these monsters. In fact, it was the acme of our hunting desires.

We read the biography of John Capen Adams and his adventures with the California grizzlies, and Roosevelt's admirable descriptions of these animals. They filled out our dreams with detail. And after killing black bears we needed only the opportunity to make our wish become an exploit.

The opportunity to do this arrived unexpectedly, as many opportunities seem to, when the want and the preparedness coincide.

The California Academy of Sciences has in its museum in Golden Gate Park, San Francisco, a collection of very fine animal habitat groups, among which are deer, antelope, mountain sheep, cougars, and brown bear. While an elk group was being installed, it happened that the taxidermist, Mr. Paul Fair, said to me that the next and final setting would be one of grizzly bears. In surprise, I asked him if it were not a fact that the California grizzly was extinct. He said this was true, but the silver-tip bear of Wyoming was a grizzly and its range extended westward to the Sierra Nevada Mountains; so it could properly be classified as a Pacific Coast variety. He cited Professor Merriam's monograph on the classification of grizzlies to prove his statements. He also informed me that permit might be obtained from Washington to secure these specimens in Yellowstone National Park.

Immediately I perceived an opportunity and interviewed Dr. Barton Everman, curator of the museum, concerning the feasibility of offering our services in taking these bears at no expense to the academy. Incidentally, we proposed to shoot them with the bow and arrow, and thereby answer a moot question in anthropology. The proposition appealed to him, and he wrote to Washington for a permit to secure specimens in this National Park, stating that the bow and arrow would be used. I insisted upon this latter stipulation, so that there should be no misunderstanding if, in the future, any objection was raised to this method of hunting.

In a very short time permit was given to the academy, and we started our preparations for the expedition. This was late in the fall of 1919, and bear were at their best in the spring, just after hibernation; so we had ample time.

It was planned that Mr. Compton, Mr. Young, and I should be the hunters, and such other assistance would be obtained as seemed necessary. We began reviewing our experience and formulating the principles of the campaign.

Our weapons we now considered adequate in the light of our contact with black bears. We had found that our bows were as strong as we could handle, and ample to drive a good arrow through a horse, a fact which we had demonstrated upon the carcasses of recently dead animals.

But we decided to add to the length of our arrowheads, and use tempered instead of soft steel as heretofore. We took particular pains to have them perfect in every detail.

Then we undertook the study of the anatomy of bears and the location and size of their vital organs. In the work of William Wright on the grizzly, we found valuable data concerning the habits and nature of these animals.

In spite of the reputation of this bear for ferocity and tenacity of life, we felt that, after all, he was only made of flesh and blood, and our arrows were capable of solving the problem.

We also began preparing ourselves for the contest. Although habitually in good physical condition, we undertook special training for the big event. By running, the use of dumbbells and other gymnastic practices, we strengthened our muscles and increased our endurance. Our field shooting was also directed toward rapid delivery and the quick judgment of distances on level, uphill, and falling ground. In fact, we planned to leave no factor for success untried.

My brother, G. D. Pope, of Detroit, being a hunter of big game with the gun, was invited to join the party, and his advice was asked concerning a reliable guide. He gladly consented to come with us and share the expenses. At the same time he suggested Ned Frost, of Cody, Wyoming, as the most experienced hunter of grizzly bears in America.

About this time one of my professional friends visited the Smithsonian Institute at Washington, where he met a member of the staff, who inquired if he knew Doctor Pope, of San Francisco, a man that was contemplating shooting grizzlies with the bow and arrow. The doctor replied that he did, whereat the sage laughed and said that the feat was impossible, most dangerous and foolhardy; it could not be done. We fully appreciated the danger involved—therein lay some of the zest. But we also knew that even should we succeed in killing them in Yellowstone Park, the glory would be sullied by the popular belief that all park bears are hotel pets, live upon garbage, and that it was a cruel shame to torment them with arrows.

So in my early correspondence with Frost, I assured him that we did not want to shoot any tame bears and that we would not consider the trip at all if this were necessary. He assured us that this was not necessary, and reminded us that Yellowstone Park was fifty miles wide by sixty miles long, and that some of the highest portions of the Rocky Mountains lay in it. The animals in this preserve, he said, were far from tame and the bears were divided into two distinct groups, one mostly composed of black and brown with a few inferior specimens of grizzlies that frequent the dumps back of the camps and hotels, and another group of bears that never came near civilization, but lived entirely up in the rugged mountains and were as dangerous and wary as those in Alaska or any other wild country. These bear wander outside the park and furnish hunting material throughout the neighboring State. He promised to put us in communication with grizzlies that were as unspoiled and unafraid as those first seen by Lewis and Clarke in their early explorations.

After explaining the purposes of our trip and the use of the bow, Ned Frost agreed that it was a real sporting proposition and took up the plan with enthusiasm. I sent him a sample arrow we used in hunting, and his letter in reply I take the liberty of printing. It is typical of the frontier spirit and comes, not only from the foremost grizzly hunter of all times, but discloses the man's bigness of heart:

"My dear Doctor:

"Your letter of the 18th was received a day or so ago, and last night I received 'Good Medicine' on the evening train, and I feel better away down deep about this hunt after a good examination of this little Grizzly Tickler than I have at any time before. I have, by mistake, let it simmer out in a quiet way that I was going to see what a grizzly would really do if he had a few sticks stuck in his innerds, and my friends have been giving the Mrs. and me a regular line of farewell parties. Really, I think it has been a splendid paying thing to do; pork chops are high, you know, and I really feel I am off to the good about nine dollars and six bits worth of bacon and flour right now on this deal. Maybe I'll be in debt to you before green-grass if I don't look out.

"Well, anyway, here is hoping we will all live through it and have a dandy time. Don't worry about coming to blows with the bear; I have noticed from long experience that it is not the times that you think a bear is going to give you trouble that it happens, but always when least expected. I have trailed wounded grizzlies time and time again, and was more or less worried all the while, but never had one turn on me yet. Then, too, I have had about three experiences with them that made my hair stand straight up, and when it finally settled, it had more FROST in it than ever before; and let me add right here, that one of the worst places I ever got into was when I had sixteen of the best bear dogs that were ever gotten together I believe, after an old she-grizzly, and I was like you, thought they would hold the bear's attention. BUT, don't let any notion like this get you into trouble. Now, I am not running down dogs as a means of getting bear; I love them and would now have a good pack if it was possible to run them in the game fields of this State, but you don't want to think that they can handle a grizzly like they do a black bear. In fact, I would place no value on them whatsoever as a safeguard in case a grizzly got on the pack, and I am speaking from experience, mind you. No, a good little shepherd would do more than a dozen regular bear dogs, but there is only about one little shepherd like I speak of in a lifetime.

"If you can use the bow from horseback, here is a safe proposition, and I believe a practical one, too. But I don't feel that there is really so much danger in the game after all, as it is only once in a great while that any bear will go up against the human animal, and then is most likely to be when you are not expecting it at all. Don't worry about it. What I am thinking about most is to get the opportunity to get the first arrow into some good big worthy old boy that will be a credit to the expedition.

"There are lots of grizzlies in the park all right, and some of them are not very wild, but if you get out away from the hotels a few miles, they are not going to come up and present their broadsides to you at thirty yards. So, as I say, I am thinking mostly about the chances of getting the opportunities. I don't know, of course, just how close you can place your arrows at thirty yards, and it is getting the first hole into them that I am most interested in now. I feel that we ought to get some good chances, as I have seen so many bear in the park; but, of course, have never hunted them and don't know just how keen they will be when it comes right down to getting their hides. There are some scattered all over the park that will rob a camp at night, and some of them will even put up a fight for it, but most of them will beat it as soon as one gets after them.

"It would be impossible, I believe, to keep dogs still while watching a bait, as they would get the scent of any approaching bear, and then you would not be able to keep them quiet, and they would most likely scare the bear out of the country. I can rustle a few dogs to take along if you want them, and pretty good dogs, too; but I am not strong for them myself only in this way, to put them on the trail of a bear and take a good horse apiece, so that we could get up to the chase and have a chance to land on him. This might be a good thing to try if all others failed.

"I know how you feel about killing clean with the bow and not having any shooting, and I can assure you that I would let 'em get just as close as you want them, and not feel any concern about their getting the best of anybody, and you would have a chance to use the bow well in this case; but I am more prone to think they will beat it off with a lot of your perfectly good arrows than anything else.

"Yours truly,
"NED FROST."

It was apparent from the first that dogs were of little use in taking grizzly. It would be necessary to shoot from blinds set conveniently near bait. Frost assured us that bears of this variety, when just out of hibernation and lean, would run out of the country if chased by a pack of dogs, and incidentally kill all that they could catch. In the fall of the year, when the bears are fat, they refuse to run, but wade through the pack, which is unable to keep him from attacking the hunter.

As an example of this, he related an instance where he started a grizzly with eight or ten Russian bear hounds, and chased the beast about thirty miles. As he followed on horseback, he found one after the other of his dogs torn to pieces, disemboweled, and dismembered. At last, he came upon the bear at bay in deep snow, against a high cliff. Only two of his hounds were left, and one of these had a broken leg. Mad with vengeance, Frost shot the grizzly. It charged him at forty yards. In quick succession he fired five bullets in the oncoming bear, seemingly with no effect. Up to his waist in the snow, he was unable to avoid its rush. It came on and fell dead on his chest, with the faithful hound hanging to it in a desperate effort to save his master.

This is one of the three or four maulings that Ned has received in his hunting experiences, which, he says, "have added frost to my golden locks." The dog became a cherished pet in the family for many years.

Frost killed his first bear when fourteen years of age, and has added nearly five hundred to this number since that time.

It is characteristic of the grizzly that he will charge upon the slightest provocation, and that nothing will turn him aside from his purpose. Later we found this particularly true where the female with cubs is concerned.

Instances of this are too well known to recount, but one coming under our own experience was related to me by Tom Murphy, the bear hunter of California.

In early days in Humboldt County, there lived an old settler named Pete Bluford, who was a squaw man. He shot a female grizzly with cubs within a quarter of a mile of what are now the town limits of Blocksburg. The beast charged and struck him to the ground. At the same time she ripped open the man's abdomen. Bluford dropped under a fallen tree, where the bear repeatedly assaulted him, tearing at his body. By rolling back and forth as the grizzly leaped over the log to reach him from the other side, he escaped further injury. Worried by the hunter's dog, she finally ceased her efforts and wandered off. The man was able to reach home in spite of a large open wound in his abdomen, with protruding intestines. This was roughly sewed together by his friend, Beany Powell. He recovered from the experience and lived many years with the Indians of that locality. As an example of Western humor, it is related that Beany Powell, when sewing up the wound with twine and a sack needle, found a large lump of fat protruding from the incision, of which he was unable to dispose; so he cut it off, tried out the grease in the frying-pan and used it to grease his boots.

Old Bluford became a character in the country. He was, in fact, what is colloquially known as "an old poison oaker." This is an individual who sinks so low in the scale of civilization that he lives out in the backwoods or poison oak brush and becomes animal in type. His hair grew to his shoulders, his beard was unkempt, his finger nails were as long as claws and filthy with dirt. Rags of unknown antiquity partially covered his limbs, vermin infested his body and he stayed with the most degraded remnants of the Indians.

One cold winter they found him dead in his dilapidated cabin. He lay on the dirt floor, his ragged coat over his face, his hands beneath his head, and two house cats lay frozen, one beneath each arm. These old pioneers were strange people and died strange deaths.

In our plans to capture grizzlies we took into consideration the proclivity of this beast to attack. We knew his speed was tremendous. He is able to catch a horse or a dog on the run. Therefore, it is useless for a man to try to run away from him. There is no such thing as being able to climb a tree if the animal is at close quarters. Adams has shown that it is a mistake to attempt it. One only stretches himself out inviting evisceration in the effort.

We decided if cornered either to dodge or to lie flat and feign death. So we practiced dodging, our running being more for the purpose of gaining endurance and to follow the bear if necessary.

Ishi, the Yana Indian, said that grizzlies were to be overcome with arrows and if they charged, they were to be met with the spear and fire. So we constructed spears having well-tempered blades more than a foot in length set upon heavy iron tubing and riveted to strong ash handles six feet in length. Back of the blade we fashioned quick lighting torches of cotton waste saturated with turpentine. These could be ignited by jerking a lanyard fastened to a spring faced with sandpaper. The spring rested on the ends of several matches. It was an ingenious and reliable device.

The Esquimaux used a long spear in hunting the polar bear. It was ten or twelve feet in length. After being shot with an arrow, if the bear charged, they rested the butt of the spear on the ground, lowered the point and let the bear impale himself on it.

When the time came to use our weapons, Ned Frost dissuaded us from the attempt. He said that he once owned a pet grizzly and kept it fast with a long chain in the back yard. This bear was so quick that it could lie in its kennel, apparently asleep, and if a chicken passed within proper distance, with incredible quickness she reached out a paw and seized the chicken without the slightest semblance of effort. And when at play, the boys tried to stick the bear with a pitchfork, she would parry the thrusts and protect herself like a boxer. It was impossible to touch her.

The fire, Frost thought, might serve at night, but in the daylight it would lose its effect. So he insisted that he would carry a gun to be used in case of attack. On our part, we stipulated that he was to resort to it only to prevent disaster and protested that such an exigency must be looked upon by us as a complete failure of our plans. We knew we could not stop the mad rush of a bear with our arrows, but we hoped to kill at least one by this means and compromise on the rest if necessary.

Indians, besides employing the spear, poisoned arrows, and fire, also used protected positions, or shot from horseback. We scorned to shoot from a tree and were told that few horses could be ridden close enough, or fast enough, to get within bowshot of a grizzly.

Inquiry among those qualified to know, led to the estimate of the number of all bears in the Park to be between five hundred and one thousand. Considering that there are some three thousand square miles of land, that there were nearly sixty thousand elk, besides hundreds of bison, antelope, mountain sheep, and similar animals, this does not seem improbable. I am aware that recent statements are to the effect that there were only forty grizzlies there. This is palpably an underestimate, and probably takes into account only those that frequent the dumps. Frost believes that there are several hundred grizzlies in the Park, many of which range out in the adjacent country. So we felt no fear of decimating their ranks, and had every hope of seeing many. In fact, their number has so increased in recent years that they have become a menace and require killing off.

During the past five years four persons have either been mauled or killed by grizzlies in Yellowstone. One of these was a teamster by the name of Jack Walsh. He was sleeping under his wagon at Cold Springs when a large bear seized him by the arm, dragged him forth and ripped open his abdomen. Walsh died of blood poison and peritonitis a few days later. Frost himself was attacked. He was conducting a party of tourists through the preserve and had just been explaining to them around the camp-fire that there was no danger of bears. He slept in the tent with a horse wrangler by the name of Phonograph Jones. In the middle of the night a huge grizzly entered his tent and stepped on the head of Jones, peeling the skin off his face by the rough pressure of his paw. The man waked with a yell, whereupon the bear clawed out his lower ribs. The cry roused Frost, who having no firearms, hurled his pillow at the bear.

With a roar, the grizzly leaped upon Ned, who dived into his sleeping bag. The animal grasped him by the thighs, and dragged him from the tent out into the forest, sleeping bag and all. As he carried off his victim, he shook him from side to side as a dog shakes a rat. Frost felt the great teeth settle down on his thigh bones and expected momentarily to have them crushed in the powerful jaws. In a thicket of jack pines over a hundred yards from camp, the bear shook him so violently that the muscles of the man's thighs tore out and he was hurled free from the bag. He landed half-naked in the undergrowth several yards away.

While the frenzied bear still worried the bedding, Frost dragged himself to a near-by pine and pulled himself up in its branches by the strength of his arms.

The camp was in an uproar; a huge fire was kindled; tin pans were beaten; one of the helpers mounted a horse and by circling around the bear, succeeded in driving him away.

After first aid measures were administered, Frost was successfully nursed back to health and usefulness by his wife. But since that time he has an inveterate hatred of grizzlies, hunting them with grim persistency.

It is said that nearly forty obnoxious grizzlies were shot by the Park rangers after this episode and Frost was given a permit to carry a weapon. We found later that he always went to sleep with a Colt automatic pistol strapped to his wrist.

We planned to enter the Park in two parties. One, comprised of Frost, the cook, horse wrangler, my brother, and his friend, Judge Henry Hulbert, of Detroit, was to proceed from Cody and come with a pack train across Sylvan Pass. Our party consisted of Arthur Young and myself; Mr. Compton was unexpectedly prevented from joining us by sickness in his family. We were to journey by rail to Ashton. This was the nearest point to Yellowstone Station on the boundary of the reservation that could be reached by railroad in winter.

We arrived at this point near the last of May 1920. The roads beyond were blocked with snow, but by good fortune, we were taken in by one of the first work trains entering the region through the personal interest and courtesy of the superintendent of the Pocatello division.

We had shipped ahead of us a quantity of provisions and came outfitted only with sleeping bags, extra clothing, and our archery equipment. This latter consisted of two bows apiece and a carrying case containing one hundred and forty-four broad-heads, the finest assembly of bows and arrows since the battle of Crecy.

Young had one newly made bow weighing eighty-five pounds and his well-tried companion of many hunts, Old Grizzly, weighing seventy-five pounds.

He later found the heavier weapon too strong for him in the cold weather of the mountains, where a man's muscles stiffen and lose their power, while his bow grows stronger.

My own bows were seventy-five pounds apiece—"Old Horrible," my favorite, a hard hitter and sweet to shoot, and "Bear Slayer," the fine-grained, crooked-limbed stave with which I helped to kill our first bear. Our arrows were the usual three-eighths birch shafts, carefully selected, straight and true. Their heads were tempered steel, as sharp as daggers. We had, of course, a few blunts and eagle arrows in the lot.

In the Park we found snow deep on the ground and the roads but recently cleared with snow plows and caterpillar tractors. We traveled by auto to Mammoth Hot Springs and paid our respects to Superintendent Albright, and ultimately settled in a vacant ranger's cabin near the Canyon. Here we awaited the coming of the second party.

Our entrance into the Park was well known to the rangers, who were instructed to give us all the assistance possible. This cabin soon became a rendezvous for them and our evenings were spent very pleasantly with stories and fireside music.

After several days, word was sent by telephone that Frost and his caravan were unable to cross Sylvan Pass because of fifty feet of snow in the defile, and that he had returned to Cody where he would take an auto truck and come around to the northern entrance to the Park, through Gardner, Montana.

At the expiration of three days he drove up to our cabin in a flurry of snow. This was about the last day in May.

Frost himself is one of the finest of Western types; born and raised in the sage brush country, a hunter of big game ever since he was large enough to hold a gun. He was in the prime of life, a man of infinite resource, courage, and fortitude. We admired him immensely.

With him he had a full camp outfit, selected after years of experience, and suited to any kind of weather.

The party consisted of Art Cunningham, the cook; G.D. Pope, and Judge Henry Hulbert. Art came equipped with a vast amount of camp craft and cookery wisdom. My brother came to see the fun, the Judge to take pictures and add dignity to the occasion. All were seasoned woodsmen and hunters.

We moved to more commodious quarters, a log cabin in the vicinity, made ourselves comfortable, and let the wind-driven snow pile deep drifts about our warm shelter while we planned a campaign against the grizzlies.

So far, we had met few bears, and these were of the tourist variety. They had stolen bacon from the elevated meat safe, and one we found in the woods sitting on his haunches calmly eating the contents of a box of soda crackers. These were the hotel pets and were nothing more than of passing interest to us.

Contrary to the usual condition, no grizzlies were to be seen. The only animals in evidence were a few half-starved elk that had wintered in the Park, marmots, and the Canadian jay birds.

We began our hunts on foot, exploring Hayden Valley, the Sour Creek region, Mt. Washburn, and the headwaters of Cascade Creek.

The ground was very wet in places and heavy with snow in the woods. It was necessary, therefore, to wear rubber pacs, a type of shoe well suited to this sort of travel.

Our party divided into two groups, usually my brother and the Judge exploring in one direction while Young and I kept close at the heels of Frost. We climbed all the high ridges and swept the country with our binocular glasses. From eight to fourteen hours a day we walked and combed the country for bear signs.

Our original plan was to bring in several decrepit old horses with the pack train and sacrifice them for bait. But because of the failure of this part of our program, we were forced to find dead elk for this purpose. We came across a number of old carcasses, but no signs that bear had visited them recently. Our first encounter with grizzly came on the fourth day. We were scouting over the country near Sulphur Mountain, when Frost saw a grizzly a mile off, feeding in a little valley. The snow had melted here and he was calmly digging roots in the soft ground. We signalled to our party and all drew together as we advanced on our first bear, keeping out of sight as we did so.

We planned to go rapidly down a little cut in the hills and intercept him as he came around the turn. Progressing at a rapid pace, Indian file, we five hunters went down the draw, when suddenly our bear, who had taken an unexpected cut-off, came walking up the ravine. At a sign from Ned, we dropped to our knees and awaited developments. The bear had not seen us and the faint breeze blew from him to us. He was about two hundred yards off. We were all in a direct line, Frost ahead, I next, Young behind me, and the others in the rear. Our bows were braced and arrows nocked.

Slowly the bear came feeding toward us. He dug the roots of white violets, he sniffed, he meandered back and forth, wholly unconscious of our presence. We hardly breathed. He was not a good specimen, rather a scrawny, long-nosed, male adolescent, but a real grizzly and would do as a starter.

At last he came within fifty yards, stopped, pawed a patch of snow, and still we did not shoot. We could not without changing our position because we were all in one line. So we waited for his next move, hoping that he would advance laterally and possibly give us a broadside exposure.

But he came onward, directly for us, and at thirty yards stopped to root in the ground again. I thought, "Now we must shoot or he will walk over us!" Just then he lifted his head and seemed to take an eyeful of Young's blue shirt. For one second he half reared and stared. I drew my bow and as the arrow left the string, he bounded up the hill. The flying shaft just grazed his shoulder, parting the fur in its course. Quick as a bouncing rubber ball, he leaped over the ground and as Young's belated arrow whizzed past him, he disappeared over the hill crest.

We rose with a deep breath and shouted with laughter. Ned said that if it had not been for that blue shirt, the bear would have bumped into us. Well, we were glad we missed him, because after all, he was not the one we were looking for. It is a hard thing to pick grizzlies to order. You can't go up and inspect them ahead of time.

This fiasco was just an encouragement to us, and we continued to rise by candle light and hunt till dark. The weather turned warmer, and the snow began to melt.

At the end of the first week we saw five grizzlies way off in the distance at the head of Hayden Valley. They were three or four miles from us and evening was approaching, so we postponed an attack on them. Next morning, bright and early, we were on the ground again, hoping to see them. Sure enough, there they were! Ned, Art and I were together; my brother and the Judge were off scouting on the other side of the ridge. It was about half past eight in the morning. The bears, four in number this time, were feeding in the grassy marshland, about three miles up the valley. Ned's motto has always been: "When you see 'em, go and get 'em."

We decided to attack immediately. Down the river bank, through the draws, up into the timber we circled at a trot. It was hard going, but we were pressed for time. At last we came out on a wooded point a quarter of a mile above the bears, and rested. We knew they were about to finish their morning feeding and go up into the forest to lay up for the day. So we watched them in seclusion.

We waxed our bowstrings and put the finishing touches on our arrow-heads with a file.

Slowly the bears mounted the foothills, heading for a large patch of snow, where Frost thought they would lie down to cool before entering the woods. It seems that their winter coat makes them very susceptible to heat, and though the sun had come out pleasantly for us, it was too hot for them. There was an old female and three half-grown cubs in their third year, all looking big enough for any museum group.

At last they settled down and began to nuzzle the snow. The time had come for action. We proposed to slip down the little ravine at the edge of the timber, cross the stream, ascend the hill on the opposite side, and come up on our quarry over the crest. We should thus be within shooting distance. The wind was right for this maneuver, so we started at once.

Now as I write my muscles quiver, my heart thumps and I flush with a strange feeling, thinking of that moment. Like a soldier before a battle, we waded into an uncharted experience. What does a man think of as he is about to enter his first grizzly encounter? I remember well what passed through my head: "Can we get there without alarming the brutes?" "How close will they be?" "Can we hit them?" "What will happen then?"

Ned Frost, Young and I were to sneak up on four healthy grizzlies in the open, and pit our nerve against their savage reaction. Ned had his rifle, but this was to be used only as a last resort, and that might easily fail at such short range.

As we walked rapidly, stepping with utmost caution, I answered all the questions of my subconscious fears. "Hit them? Why, we will soak them in the gizzard; wreck them!" "Charge? Let them come on and may the best man win!" "Die? There never was a fairer, brighter, better day to die on." In fact, "Lead on!" I felt absolutely gay. A little profanity or a little intellectual detachment at these times is of material help in the process of auto-suggestion.

As for Young, he was silent, and possibly was thinking of camp flapjacks.

Half way up the hill, on the opposite side of which lay our grizzlies, we stopped, braced our bows, took three arrows apiece from our quivers, and proceeded in a more stealthy approach.

Young and I arranged ourselves on each side of Frost, abreast with him. Near the top Ned took out a green silk handkerchief and floated it in the gentle breeze to see if the wind had changed. If it had, we might find the bears coming over the top to meet us. Everything was perfect, so far! Now, stooping low we crept to the very ridge itself, to a spot directly above which we believed the bears to be. Laying our hats on the grass and sticking our extra arrows in the ground before us, we rose up, bows half drawn, ready to shoot.

There on the snow, not over twenty-five yards off, lay four grizzly bears, just like so many hearth rugs.

Instantly, I selected the farthest bear for my mark and at a signal of the eye we drew our great bows to their uttermost and loosed two deadly arrows.

We struck! There was a roar, they rose, but instead of charging us, they rushed together and began such a fight as few men have seen. My bear, pinioned with an arrow in the shoulder, threw himself on his mother, biting her with savage fury. She in turn bit him in the bloody shoulder and snapped my arrow off short. Then all the cubs attacked her. The growls and bellowing were terrific.

Quickly I nocked another arrow. The beasts were milling around together, pawing, biting, mad with rage. I shot at my bear and missed him. I nocked again. The old she-bear reared on her haunches, stood high above the circling bunch, cuffing and roaring, the blood running from her mouth and nostrils in frothy streams. Young's arrow was deep in her chest. I drove a feathered shaft below her foreleg.

The confusion and bellowing increased, and, as I drew a fourth arrow from my quiver, I glanced up just in time to see the old female's hair rise on the back of her neck. She steadied herself in her wild hurtling and looked directly at us with red glaring eyes. She saw us for the first time! Instinctively I knew she would charge, and she did.

Quick as thought, she bounded toward us. Two great leaps and she was on us. A gun went off at my ear. The bear was literally knocked head over heels, and fell in backward somersaults down the steep snowbank. At some fifty yards she checked her course, gathered herself, and attempted to charge again, but her right foreleg failed her. She rose on her haunches in an effort to advance, when, like a flash, two arrows flew at her and disappeared through her heaving sides. She faltered, wilted, and as we drew to shoot again, she sprawled out on the ground, a convulsed, quivering mass of fur and muscle—she was dead.

The half grown cubs had disappeared at the boom of the gun. We saw one making off at a gallop, three hundred yards away. The glittering snowbank before us was vacant.

The air seemed strangely still; the silence was oppressive. Our nervous tension exploded in a wave of laughter and exclamations of wonderment. Frost declared he had never seen such a spectacle in all his life; four grizzly bears in deadly combat; the din of battle; the wild bellowing; and two bowmen shooting arrow after arrow into this jumble of struggling beasts.

The snow was trampled and soaked with blood as though there had been an Indian massacre. We paced off the distance at which the charging female had been stopped. It was exactly eight yards. A mighty handy shot!

We went down to view the remains. Young had three arrows in the old bear, one deep in her neck, its point emerging back of the shoulder. He shot that as she came at us. His first arrow struck anterior to her shoulder, entered her chest, and cut her left lung from top to bottom. His third arrow pierced her thorax, through and through, and lay on the ground beside her with only its feathers in the wound.

My first arrow cut below the diaphragm, penetrated the stomach and liver, severed the gall ducts and portal vein. My second arrow passed completely through her abdomen and lay on the ground several yards beyond her. It had cut the intestines in a dozen places and opened large branches of the mesenteric artery.

The bullet from Frost's gun had entered at the right shoulder, fractured the humerus, blown a hole an inch in diameter in the chest wall, opened up a jagged hole in the trachea, and dissipated its energy in the left lung. No wound of exit was found, the soft nose copper-jacketed bullet apparently having gone to pieces after striking the bone.

Anatomically speaking, it was an effective shot, knocked the bear down and crippled her, but was not an immediately fatal wound. We had her killed with arrows, but she did not know it. She undoubtedly would have been right on us in another second. The outcome of this hypothetical encounter I leave to those with vivid imaginations.

We hereby express our gratitude to Ned Frost.

Now one of us had to rush off and get the rest of the party. Judge Hulbert and my brother were in another valley in quest of bear. So Ned set off at a rapid tramp across the bogs, streams, and hills to find them. Within an hour they returned together to view the wreckage. Photographs were taken, the skinning and autopsy were performed. Then we looked around for the wounded cub. Frost trailed him by almost invisible blood stains and tracks, and found him less than a quarter of a mile away, huddled up as if asleep on the hillside, my arrow nestled to his breast. The broken shaft with its blade deep in the thorax had completely severed the head of his humerus, cut two ribs, and killed him by hemorrhage from the pulmonary arteries. Half-grown as he was, he would have made an ugly antagonist for any man.

His mother, a fine mature lady of the old school, showed by her teeth and other lineaments her age and respectability. In autumn she would have weighed four or five hundred pounds. We weighed her in installments with our spring scales; she registered three hundred and five pounds. She was in poor condition and her pelt was not suitable for museum purposes. But these features could not be determined readily beforehand. The juvenile Ursus weighed one hundred and thirty-five pounds. We measured them, gathered their bones for the museum, shouldered their hides, and turned back to camp.

That night Ned Frost said, "Boys, when you proposed shooting grizzly bears with the bow and arrow, I thought it a fine sporting proposition, but I had my doubts about its success. Now I know that you can shoot through and kill the biggest grizzly in Wyoming!"

Our instructions on leaving California were to secure a large male *Ursus Horribilis Imperator*, a good representative female, and two or three cubs. The female we had shot filled the requirements fairly well, but the two-year-old cub was at the high school age and hardly cute enough to be admired. Moreover, no sooner had we sent the news of our first success to the Museum than we were informed that this size cub was not wanted and that we must secure little ones.

So we set out to get some of this year's vintage in small bears. Ordinarily, there is no difficulty in coming in contact with bears in Yellowstone; in fact, it is more common to try to keep some of the hotel variety from eating at the same table with you. But not a single bear, black, brown, or silver-tipped, now called upon us. We traveled all over that beautiful Park, from Mammoth Hot Springs to the Lake. We hunted over every well-known bear district. Tower Falls, Specimen Ridge, Buffalo Corrals, Mt. Washburn, Dunraven Pass (under twenty-five feet of snow), Antelope Creek, Pelican Meadows, Cub Creek, Steamboat Point, and kept the rangers busy on the lookout for bear. From eight to fifteen hours a day we hunted. We walked over endless miles of mountains, climbed over countless logs, plowed through snow and slush, and raked the valleys with our field glasses.

But bears were as scarce as hen's teeth. We saw a few tracks but nothing compared to those seen in other years.

We began to have a sneaking idea that the bear had all been killed off. We knew they had been a pest to campers and were becoming a menace to human life. We suspected the Park authorities of quiet extermination. Several of the rangers admitted that a selective killing was carried out yearly to rid the preserve of the more dangerous individuals.

Then the elk began to pour back into the Park; singly, in couples, and in droves they returned, lean and scraggly. A few began to drop their calves. Then we began to see bear signs. The grizzly follow the elk, and after they come out of hibernation and get their fill of green grass, they naturally take to elk calves. Occasionally they include the mother in the menu.

We also began to follow the elk. We watched at bait. We sat up nights and days at a time, seeing only a few unfavorable specimens and these were as wild and as wary as deer. We found the mosquitoes more deadly than the bear. We tracked big worthy old boys around in circles and had various frustrated encounters with she-bears and cubs.

Upon one occasion we were tracking a prospective specimen through the woods, proceeding with great caution, when evidently the beast heard us. Suddenly, he turned on his tracks and came on a dead run for us. I was in advance and instantly drew my bow, holding it for the right moment to shoot. The bear came directly in our front, not more than twenty yards away and being startled by the sight of us, threw his locomotive mechanism into reverse and skidded towards us in a cloud of snow and forest leaves. In the fraction of a second, I perceived that he was afraid and not a proper specimen for our use. I held my arrow and the bear with an indignant and disgusted look, made a precipitous retreat. It was an unexpected surprise on both sides.

They say that the Indians avoided the Yellowstone region, thinking it a land of evil spirits. In our wanderings, however, we picked up on Steamboat Point a beautiful red chert arrow-head, undoubtedly shot by an Indian at elk years before Columbus burst in upon these good people. In Hayden Valley we found an obsidian spear head, another sign that the Indian knew good hunting grounds.

But no Indian was ever so anxious to meet grizzly as we were. We hunted continually, but found none that suited us; we had to have the best. Frost assured us that we had made a mistake in ever trying to get grizzlies in the Park—and that in the time we spent there we could have secured all our required specimens in the game fields of Wyoming or Montana.

A month passed; the bears were beginning to lose their winter coats; our party began to disintegrate. My brother and the Judge were compelled to return to Detroit. A week or so later Ned Frost and the cook were scheduled to take out another party of hunters from Cody and prepared to leave us. Young and I were determined to stick it out until the last chance was exhausted. We just had to get those specimens.

Before Frost left us, however, he packed us up to the head of Cascade Creek with our bows and arrows, bed rolls, a tarpaulin, and a couple of boxes of provisions.

We had received word from a ranger that a big old grizzly had been seen at Soda Butte and we prepared to go after him. At the last moment before departure, a second word came that probably this same bear had moved down to Tower Falls and was ranging between this point and the Canyon, killing elk around Dunraven Pass.

Young and I scouted over this area and found diggings and his tracks.

A good-sized bear will have a nine-inch track. This monster's was eleven inches long. We saw where he made his kills and used certain fixed trails going up and down the canyons.

Frost gave us some parting advice and his blessing, consigned us to our fate, and went home.

Left to ourselves, we two archers inspected our tackle and put everything in prime condition. Our bows had stood the many wettings well, but we oiled them again. New strings were put on and thoroughly waxed. Our arrows were straightened, their feathers dried and preened in the sun. The broad-heads were set on straight and sharpened to the last degree, and so prepared we determined to do our utmost. We were ready for the big fellow.

In our reconnaissance we found that he was a real killer. His trail was marked by many bloody episodes. It seemed quite probable that he was the bear that two years before burst in upon a party of surveyors in the mountains and kept them treed all night. It is not unlikely that he was the same bear that caused the death of Jack Walsh. He seemed too expert in planning murder. We saw by his tracks how he lay in ambush watching a herd of elk, how he sneaked up on a mother elk and her recently born calf on the outskirts of the band, and with a great leap threw himself upon the two and killed them.

In several places we saw the skins of these little wapiti licked clean and empty of bodily structure. No other male grizzly was permitted to enter his domain. He was, in fact, the monarch of the mountain, the great bear of Dunraven Pass.

We pitched our little tent in a secluded wood some three miles from the lake at the head of Cascade Creek, and began to lay our plan of attack. We were by this time inured to fatigue and disappointment. Weariness and loss of sleep had produced a dogged determination that knew no relaxation. And yet we were cheerful. Young has that fine quality so essential to a hunting companion, imperturbable good nature, never complaining, no matter how heavy the load, how long the trail, how late or how early the hour, how cold, how hot, how little, or how poor the food.

We were there to win and nothing else mattered. If it rained and we must wait, we took out our musical instruments, built up the fire and soothed our troubled souls with harmony. This is better than tobacco or whiskey for the purpose. In fact, Young is so abstemious that even tea or coffee seem a bit intemperate to him, and are only to be used under great physical strain; and as for profanity, why, I had to do all the swearing for the two of us.

We were trained down to rawhide and sinew, keyed to alertness and ready for any emergency.

Often in our wanderings at night we ran unexpectedly upon wild beasts in the dark. Some of these were bears. Our pocket flashlights were used as defensive weapons. A snort, a crashing retreat through the brush told us that our visitant had departed in haste, unable to stand the glaring light of modern science.

We soon found that our big fellow was a night rover also, and visited his various kills under the cloak of darkness. In one particularly steep and rugged canyon, he crossed a little creek at a set place. Up on the side of this canyon he mounted to the plateau above by one of three possible trails. At the top within forty yards of one of these was a small promontory of rock upon which we decided to form a blind and await his coming. We fashioned a shelter of young jack pines, constructed like a miniature corral, less than three by six feet in area, but very natural in appearance. Between us and the trail was a quantity of down timber which we hoped would act as an impediment to an onrushing bear. And the perpendicular face of our outcropping elevated us some twelve or thirteen feet above the steep hillside. A small tree stood near our position and offered a possibility in case of attack. But we had long ago decided that no man can clamber up a tree in time to escape a grizzly charging at a distance less than fifty yards. We could be approached from the rear, but altogether it was an ideal ambush.

The wind blew steadily up the canyon all night long and carried our scent away from the trail. Above us on the plateau was a recently killed elk which acted as a perpetual invitation to bears and other prowlers of the night.

So we started watching in this blind, coming soon after dusk and remaining until sunrise. The nights were cold, the ground pitiless, and the moon, nearly at its full, crept low through a maze of mist.

Dressed in our warmest clothing and permitting ourselves one blanket and a small piece of canvas, we huddled together in a cramped posture and kept vigil through the long hours. Neither of us smoked anyway, and of course, this was absolutely taboo; we hardly whispered, and even shifted our positions with utmost caution. Before us lay our bows ready strung, and arrows, both in the quiver belted upright to the screen and standing free close at hand.

The first evening we saw an old she-bear and her two-year-old cubs come up the path. They passed us with that soft shuffling gait so uncanny to hear in the dark. We were delighted that they showed no sign of having detected us. But they were not suited to our purpose and we let them go. The female was homely, fretful and nervous. The cubs were yellow and ungainly. We looked for better things.

Bears have personality, as obvious as humans. Some are lazy, some alert, surly, or timid. Nearly all the females we saw showed that irritability and irascible disposition that go with the cares of maternity. This family was decidedly commonplace.

They disappeared in the gloom, and we waited and waited for the big fellow that some time must appear.

But morning came first; we stole from our blind, chilled and stiffened, and wandered back to camp to breakfast and sleep. The former was a fairly successful event, but the latter was made almost impossible by the swarms of mosquitoes that beset us. A smudge fire and canvas head-coverings gave us only a partial immunity. By sundown we were on our way again to the blind, but another cold dreary night passed without adventure.

On our way to camp in the dim light of early dawn, a land fog hung low in the valley. As we came up a rough path there suddenly appeared out of the obscurity three little bear cubs, not thirty-five yards away. They winded us, squeaked and stood on their hind legs, peering in our direction. We dropped like stones in our tracks, scarcely breathing, figuratively frozen to the ground, for instantly the fiercest-looking grizzly we ever saw bounded over the cubs and straddled them between her forelegs. Nothing could stop her if she came on. A little brush intervened and she could not locate us plainly for we could see her eyes wander in search of us; but her trembling muscles, the vicious champing of her jaws, and the guttural growls, all spoke of immediate attack. We were petrified. She wavered in her intent, turned, cuffed her cubs down the hill, snorted and finally departed with her family.

We heaved a deep sigh of relief. But she was wonderful, she was the most beautiful bear we had ever seen; large, well proportioned, with dark brown hair having just a touch of silver. She was a patrician, the aristocrat of the species. We marked her well.

Next day, just at sunset, we got our first view of the great bear of Dunraven Pass. He was coming down a distant canyon trail. He looked like a giant in the twilight. With long swinging strides he threw himself impetuously down the mountainside. Great power was in every movement. He was magnificent! He seemed as large as a horse, and had that grand supple strength given to no other predatory animal

Though we were used to bears, a strange misgiving came over me. We proposed to slay this monster with the bow and arrow. It seemed preposterous!

In the blind another long cold night passed. The moon drifted slowly across the heavens and sank in a haze of clouds at daybreak. Just at the hush of dawn, the homely female and her tow-headed progeny came shuffling by. We were desperate for specimens, and one of these would match that which we already had. I drew up my bow and let fly a broadhead at one of the cubs. It struck him in the ribs. Precipitately, the whole band took flight. My quarry fell against an obstructing log and died. His mother stopped, came back several times, gazed at him pensively, then disappeared. We got out, carried him to a distant spot and skinned him. He weighed one hundred and twenty pounds. My arrow had shaved a piece off his heart. Death was instantaneous.

We packed home the hind quarters and made a fine grizzly stew. Before this we had found that the old bears were tough and rancid, but the little ones were as sweet and tender as suckling pigs. This stew was particularly good, well seasoned with canned tomatoes and the last of our potatoes and onions. Sad to relate the better part of this savory pot next day was eaten by a wandering vagabond of the *Ursus* family. Not content with our stew, he devoured all our sugar, bacon, and other foodstuffs not in cans, and wound up his debauch by wiping his feet on our beds and generally messing up the camp. Probably he was a regular camp thief.

That night, early in the watch, we heard the worthy old boy come down the canyon, hot in pursuit of a large brown bear. As he ran, the great animal made quite a noise. His claws clattered on the rocks, and the ground seemed to shake beneath us. We shifted our bows ready for action, and felt the keen edge of our arrows. Way off in the forest we heard him tree the cowardly intruder with such growls and ripping of bark that one would imagine he was about to tear the tree down.

After a long time he desisted and, grunting and wheezing, came slowly up the canyon. With the night glasses we could see him. He seemed to be considerably heated with his exercise and scratched himself against a young fir tree. As he stood on his hind legs with his back to the trunk and rubbed himself to and fro, the tree swayed like a reed; and as he lifted his nose I observed that it just touched one of the lower branches. In the morning, after he had gone and we were on our way to camp, we passed this very fir and stretching up on my tip toes, I could just touch the limb with my fingers. Having been a pole vaulter in my youth, I knew by experience that this measurement was over seven feet six inches. He was a real he-bear! We wanted him more than ever.

The following day it rained—in fact, it rained nearly every day near the end of our stay; but this was a drenching that stopped at sunset, leaving all the world sweet and fragrant. The moon came out full and beautiful, everything seemed propitious.

We went to the blind about an hour before midnight, feeling that surely this evening the big fellow would come. After two hours of frigidity and immobility, we heard the velvet footfalls of bear coming up the canyon. There came our patrician and her royal family. The little fellows pattered up the trail before their mother. They came within range. I signalled Young and we shot together at the cubs. We struck. There was a squeak, a roar, a jumble of shadowy figures and the entire flock of bears came tumbling in our direction.

At that very moment the big grizzly appeared on the scene. There were five bears in sight. Turning her head from side to side, trying to find her enemy, the she-bear came towards us. I whispered to Young, "Shoot the big fellow." At the same time, I drew an arrow to the head, and drove it at the oncoming female. It struck her full in the chest. She reared; threw herself sidewise, bellowed with rage, staggered and fell to the ground. She rose again, weakened, stumbled forward, and with great gasps she died. In less than half a minute it was all over. The little ones ran up the hill past us, one later returned and sat up at its mother's head, then disappeared in the dark forever.

While all this transpired, the monster grizzly was romping back and forth in the shaded forest not more than sixty-five yards away. With deep booming growls like distant thunder, he voiced his anger and intent to kill. As he flitted between the shadows of the trees, the moonlight glinted on his massive body; he was enormous.

Young discharged three arrows at him. I shot two. We should have landed, he was so large. But he galloped off and I saw my last arrow at the point blank range of seventy-five yards, fall between his legs. He was gone. We thought we had missed the beast and grief descended heavy upon us. The thought of all the weary days and nights of hunting and waiting, and now to have lost him, was very painful.

After our palpitating hearts were quiet and the world seemed peaceful, we got out of our blind and skinned the female by flashlight. She was a magnificent specimen, just right in color and size for the Museum, not fat, but weighing a trifle over five hundred pounds. My arrow had severed a rib and buried its head in her heart. We measured her and saved her skull and long bones for the taxidermist.

At daybreak we searched for the cubs and found one dead under a log with an arrow through his brain. The others had disappeared.

We had no idea that we hit the great bear, but just to gather up our shafts, we went over the ground where he had been.

One of Young's arrows was missing!

That gave us a thrill; perhaps we had hit him after all! We went further in the direction he had gone; there was a trace of blood.

We trailed him. We knew it was dangerous business. Through clumps of jack pines we cautiously followed, peering under every pile of brush and fallen tree. Deep into the forest we tracked him, where his bloody smear was left upon fallen logs. Soon we found where he had rested. Then we discovered the fore part of Young's arrow. It had gone through him. There was a pool of blood. Then we found the feathered butt which he had drawn out with his teeth.

Four times he wallowed down in the mud or soft earth to rest and cool his wound. Then beneath a great fir he had made a bed in the soft loam and left it. Past this we could not track him. We hunted high and low, but no trace of him could we find. Apparently he had ceased bleeding and his footprints were not recorded on the stony ground about. We made wide circles, hoping to pick up his trail. We searched up and down the creek. We cross-cut every forest path and runway, but no vestige remained.

He was gone. We even looked up in the tree and down in the ground where he had wallowed. For five hours we searched in vain, and at last, worn with disappointment and fatigue, we lay down and slept on the very spot where he last stopped.

Near sundown we awoke, ate a little food, and started all over again to find the great bear. We retraced our steps and followed the fading evidence till it brought us again to the pit beneath the fir tree. He must be near. It was absolutely impossible for any animal to have lost so much blood and travel more than a few hundred yards past this spot. We had explored the creek bottom and the cliffs above from below, and we now determined to traverse every foot of the rim of the canyon from above. As we climbed over the face of the rock we saw a clot of dried blood. We let ourselves down the sheer descent, came upon a narrow little ledge, and there below us lay the huge monster on his back, against a boulder, cold and stiff, as dead as Cesar. Our hearts nearly burst with happiness.

There lay the largest grizzly bear in Wyoming, dead at our feet. His rugged coat was matted with blood. Well back in his chest the arrow wound showed clear. I measured him; twenty-six inches of bear had been pierced through and through. One arrow killed him. He was tremendous. His great wide head; his worn, glistening teeth; his massive arms; his vast, ponderous feet and long curved claws; all were there. He was a wonderful beast. It seemed incredible. I thumped Young on the shoulder: "My, that was a marvelous shot!"

We started to skin our quarry. It was a stupendous job, as he weighed nearly one thousand pounds, and lay on the steep canyon side ready to roll on and crush us. But with ropes we lashed him by the neck to a tree and split him up the back, later box-skinning the legs according to the method required by the museum.

By flashlight, acetylene lamp, candle light, fire light and moonlight, we labored. We used up all our knives, and having neglected to bring our whet-stones, sharpened our blades on the volcanic boulders, about us. By assiduous industry for nine straight hours, we finished him after a fashion. His skin was thick and like scar tissue. His meat was all tendons and gristle. The hide was as tight as if glued on.

In the middle of the night we stopped long enough to broil some grizzly cub steaks and brew a pot of tea; then we went at it again.

As we dismembered him we weighed the parts. The veins were absolutely dry of blood, and without this substance, which represents a loss of nearly 10 per cent of his weight, he was nine hundred and sixteen pounds. There was hardly an inch of fat on his back. At the end of the autumn this adipose layer would be nearly six inches thick. He would then have weighed over fourteen hundred pounds. He stood nearly four feet high at the shoulders, while his skull measured eighteen and a half inches long; his entire body length was seven feet four inches.

As we cleaned his bones we hurled great slabs of muscle down the canyon, knowing from experience that this would be a sign for all other bears to leave the vicinity. Only the wolves and jays will eat grizzly meat.

At last we finished him, as the sun rose over the mountain ridges and gilded all the canyon with glory. We cleaned and salted the pelts, packed them on our backs, and, dripping with salt brine and bear grease, staggered to the nearest wagon trail. The hide of the big bear, with unskinned paws and skull, weighed nearly one hundred and fifty pounds.

We cached our trophies, tramped the weary miles back to camp, cleaned up, packed and wandered to the nearest station, from which we ordered a machine. When this arrived we gathered our belongings, turned our various specimens over to a park ranger, to be given the final treatments, and started on our homeward trip.

We were so exhausted from loss of sleep, exertion and excitement, that we sank into a stupor that lasted almost the entire way home.

The California Academy of Sciences now has a handsome representative group of *Ursus Horribilis Imperator*. We have the extremely satisfactory feeling that we killed five of the finest grizzly bear in Wyoming. The sport was fair and clean, and we did it all with the bow and arrow.

XV

ALASKAN ADVENTURES

It seems as if Fate had chosen my hunting companion, Arthur Young, to add to the honor and the legends of the bow. At any rate it fell to his lot to make two trips to Alaska between the years 1922 and 1925.

He and his friend, Jack Robertson, were financed in a project to collect moving-picture scenes of the Northland.

They were instructed to show the country in all its seasonal phases, to depict the rivers, forests, glaciers and mountains, particularly to record the summer beauties of Alaska. The animal life was to be featured in full:—fish, birds, small game, caribou, mountain sheep, moose and bear, all were to be captured on the celluloid film, and with all this a certain amount of hunting with the bow was to be included and the whole woven into a little story of adventure.

Equipped with cameras, camp outfit and archery tackle, they sailed for Seward. From here they ventured into the wilderness as circumstances directed. Sometimes they went by boat to Kadiac Island, sometimes to the Kenai Peninsula, or they journeyed by dog sleds and packs inland. They spent the better part of two years in this hard, exacting work, often carrying as much as a hundred pounds on their backs for many miles. Great credit must be given to Art's partner Jack Robertson, for his energy, bravery and fortitude. His work with the camera will make history, but for the time being we shall focus our attention on the man with the bow. Only a small portion of Young's time was devoted to hunting, the exigencies incidental to travel and gathering animal pictures were such that archery was of secondary importance.

He hunted and shot ptarmigan, some on the wing; he added grouse and rabbit meat to the scant larder of their "go light" outfit. He shot graylings and salmon in the streams. He could easily have killed caribou because they operated close to vast herds of these foolish beasts. However, at the time it seemed that there was no hurry about the matter; they had meat in camp, and pictures were of greater interest just then. They expected to see plenty of these animals. Strangely enough the herd suddenly left the country and no further opportunity presented itself for shooting them. This was no great disappointment because the sport was too easy. What did seem worth while was the killing of the great Alaskan moose. These beasts are the largest game animal on this continent, with the exception of the almost extinct bison.

Young had his first chance at moose while on the Kenai Peninsula. Here the boys were camped and having finished his camera work Art took a day off to hunt.

In the afternoon he discovered a large old bull lying down in a burnt-over area, where approach by stealth was possible, so he began his stalk with utmost caution, paying particular attention to scent and sound. By crawling on his hands and knees he came within a hundred and fifty yards, when his progress was stopped by a fallen tree. To go around it, would expose him to vision; to climb over, would alarm the animal by snapping twigs; so Young decided to dig under. He worked with his hunting knife and hands for one hour to accomplish this operation. When he had passed this obstacle he continued his crawling till he reached a distance of sixty yards. At this stage Art called the old bull with a birch bark horn, then the moose heard him and stood up. The brush was so thick that he could not shoot immediately, but waited as the old bull circled to catch his wind and answered the challenge. When he presented a fair target at seventy yards or so, Art drove an arrow at him. It struck deep in the flank, up to the feather ranging forward. The bull was only startled a trifle and trotted off a hundred yards. Here he stopped to look and listen. Young drew his bow again, and overshooting his mark, his arrow struck one of the broad thick palms of the antlers. The point pierced the two inches of bone and wedged tight, making a sharp report as it hit. This started the animal off at a fast trot. Young followed slowly at some distance and soon had the satisfaction of seeing the moose waver in his course and lie down. After a reasonable wait the hunter advanced to his quarry and found him dead. The triumph of such an episode is more or less mixed with misery. The pleasure undoubtedly would have been greater had some other lusty bow man been with him, but as it was he had to feast his eyes alone, moreover he had to make his way back to camp, which was some eight miles off, and night rapidly coming on.

This part of the story was just as thrilling to Art, because he must stumble through the rough land of "little sticks" in the dark with the constant apprehension of meeting some unwelcome Alaska brown bear, which were thick there, and also the extremely unpleasant experience of running into dead trees, tripping over fallen limbs and dropping into gullies. He reached camp ultimately, I believe. Next day he returned with his companion for meat, his antler trophy and the picture, which we present.

This bull weighed approximately sixteen hundred pounds and had a spread of sixty inches across its antlers.

Upon the second expedition a year later, Young bagged another moose. Here the arrow penetrated both sides of the chest and caused almost instant death, showing that size is not a hindrance to a quick exodus.

It is surprising even to us to see the extreme facility with which an arrow can interrupt the essential physiological processes of life and destroy it. We have come to the belief that no beast is too tough or too large to be slain by an arrow. With especially constructed heads sharpened to the utmost nicety, I have shot through a double thickness of elephant hide, two inches of cardboard, a bag of shaving and gone into an inch of wood. We feel sure that having penetrated the hide of a pachyderm his ribs can easily be severed and the heart or pulmonary cavity entered. Any considerable incision of either of these vital areas must soon cause death. And this is a field experiment which we propose to try in the near future.

There is a legitimate excuse for shooting animals such as moose, where food is a problem and the bow bears an honorable part in the episode. We feel moreover that by using the bow on this large game we are playing ultimately for game preservation. For by shaming the "mighty hunter" and his unfair methods in the use of powerful destructive agents, we feel that we help to develop better sporting ethics.

It was partly on this account, and partly to answer the dare of those who have said, "You may hunt the tame bears of California and Wyoming, but you cannot fool with the big Kadiac bears of Alaska with your little bow and arrow," that Young determined to go after these monsters and see if they were as fierce and invulnerable as claimed. At the present writing we who shoot the bow have slain more than a dozen bears with our shafts, but the mighty Kadiac brown grizzly has laughed at us from his frozen lair—as the literary nature fakir might say—we have been told that all that is necessary if you wish to meet a brownie, is to give him your address in Alaska and he will look you up. Also we have been told that once insulted he will tear a house down to "get even with you,"—so I shook Art's hand good-bye, when he started on this Kadiac escapade, and told him to "give 'em hell."

After a long time he came back to San Francisco, and this is the story he told me—and Art has no guile in his system but is as straight as a bowstring.

"We made a false start in going after our bears. We took a boat from Seward and sailed to Seldie, then to Kenai Peninsula. Here we hunted for two solid weeks and found practically no signs of brownies.

"I decided at the end of this period to waste no more time, but to pull out of the country and sail back to Seward. We had but a short time to complete our picture before the last boat left the Arctic waters, but hearing of good bear signs on Kadiac Island we hit out for this place and landed in Uganik Bay. Here in the Long Arm, we found a country with many streams flowing down from the mountains which constitute this Island, and much small timber in combination with open grassy glades. A type of country that is particularly suited for photographic work and bow hunting.

"After several days' exploring we discovered that the bears were catching salmon in the streams and we were successful in photographing as many as seven grizzlies at once. We took pictures of the bears wading in the water looking for fish. Usually the bear slaps the salmon out of the stream, then goes up on the bank and eats it. The "humpies" were so plentiful here, however, that they were tossed out on the bank, but not eaten, the bear preferring to capture one while in the water then wade about on his hind legs while he held the fish in his arms and devoured it.

"We got all this and many comic antics of young bears climbing trees and playing about by using a telephoto lens. After the camera man was satisfied I proposed that we 'pull off' a 'stunt' with the bow.

"By good fortune we saw four bears coming down the mountain side to fish. They were making their way slowly through an open valley. The camera was stationed at a commanding point and I ran up a dry wash thickly grown with willow and alder to head off the bears. I was able to get within a hundred yards by use of the willow cover, then the brush became too thin to hide me, so I walked boldly out into the open to meet the bears. I practically invited them to charge since they were reputed to be so easily insulted. At first they paid little attention to me, then the two in advance sat up on their haunches in astonishment and curiosity. I approached to a distance of fifty yards, then the largest brownie began champing his jaws and growling; then he 'pinned back his ears' preparing to come at me. Just as he was about to lunge forward I shot him in the chest. The arrow went deep and stuck out a foot beyond his shoulder. He dropped on all fours and before he could make up his mind what hit him, I shot him again in the flank. This turned him and feeling himself badly wounded he wheeled about and ran. While this was going on an old female also stood in a menacing attitude, but as the wounded bear galloped past her, she came to the ground and ran diagonally from us. All of them followed suit, and as they swept out of the field of vision the wounded bear weakened and fell less than a hundred yards from the camera.

"True to his standards the camera man continued to grind out the film to the very last, so the whole picture is complete. You will see it some day for yourself and it will answer all doubts about the invulnerable status of the Kadiac bears."

Young himself was not particularly elated over this conquest. He knew long ago that the Kadiac bear was no more formidable than the grizzlies we had slain and he only undertook this adventure for show purposes. Moreover though he used his heavy osage orange bow and usual broad-heads, he declares that he believes he can kill the largest bear in Alaska with a fifty pound weapon and proportionately adjusted arrows. Both Young and I are convinced of the necessity of very sharp broad-heads, and trust more to a keen blade and a quick flight than to power.

During his Alaskan travels Art preferred his Osage bows to the yew. They stood being dragged over rocks and falling down mountain sides better than the softer yew wood. His three bows were under five feet six inches in length, short for convenience and each pulled over eighty-five pounds. The country in which he worked was so rocky that it was most disastrous on arrows, and every shot that missed meant a shattered shaft.

Possibly his roughest trip was one taken to picture mountain goats. Here a funny incident occurred. Jack and Art were stalking a herd of these wary creatures with the camera when suddenly around a point of rock the whole band of goats appeared. Art was ahead and had only just time enough to duck down on his hands and knees and hide his face close to the ground. He stayed so still that the entire flock passed close by him almost touching his body, while the camera man did his work from a concealed ledge higher up. Though Young counts it little to his credit, he shot one of these male goats, which was poised on so precipitous a point that it fell over and over down the mountain side and was lost as a trophy and as camp meat. Humiliating as such an episode may be, it serves, however, to add a coup to the archer's count. And there we let the matter rest.

But what is of greater interest is his outwitting a Rocky Mountain Big Horn. This animal is considered the greatest game trophy in America. It is an extremely alert sheep, all eyes and wisdom. If you expose yourself but a second, though you be a mile away from the ram, probably you will be seen. And though the sheep may not move while you look at him, he is gone when you have completed your toilsome climb and peer over the last ledge of rock preparatory to shooting. Ned Frost used to say that when he hunted Big Horns he paid no attention to hearing or smell, but he was so careful about sight, that when he raised his head cautiously over a ridge to observe the sheep, he always lifted a stone and peered underneath it, or picked up a bunch of grass and gazed through it.

Most hunters are content to stalk this game within three or four hundred yards, then aim at it with telescopic sights. It is the last word in good hunting.

Stewart Edward White, the author and big game hunter, has said that the following experience is one of the finest demonstrations of stalking and understanding of animal psychology he knows.

Up near the head of Wood River, Young and his party came on a number of Big Horn Sheep and first devoted several days to film work. Then Young decided to try for a trophy with the bow. After hunting all morning he discovered with his glasses a ram a long way off.

The country was open and had no cover. The ram was resting on a ledge of rock elevated above the level of the valley. Even at a distance of half a mile it was evident to Art that the ram had seen him, so Young studied the sheep and the country carefully before deciding what plan to pursue.

From the lay of the land it was plain that no concealment was possible and no detour or ambush could be employed. The glasses showed that the ram was a fairly old specimen and had a very sophisticated look. In fact, to Art he looked conceited and had an expression that said: "There is a man, but I am a pretty wise old sheep; I know all about men; that fellow hasn't seen me yet and when he does, there is plenty of open country back of me; my best plan is to lie still and let this tenderfoot pass." So he went on ruminating and blinking at the sun.

Taking this mental attitude into consideration, Young decided that the best method of outwitting this particular sheep was to take him at his own valuation and proceed as a tenderfoot down the valley. So he walked unconcernedly along at an oblique angle to the sheep and never once taking a direct look at him. He went gaily along whistling, kicking pebbles and swinging his bow. When he had reached a distance of two or three hundred yards the old sheep lifted up his head to see what was going on. Young paid no attention to him, though he observed him out of the corner of his eyes. So the wise old boy settled back content with his diagnosis.

Art walked along as innocently as ever. When he was a hundred and fifty yards off, the ram raised his head again and took a longer observation. He seemed to be changing his mind. Young said to himself, "He will take one more look, then he will go. Now is the time to act." So nocking an arrow on the string he ran at full speed directly at the sheep, and when half way he saw the tip of his horns rise above the ledge and knew it was time to stop. He came to his shooting pose and waited, the arrow half drawn. Sure enough! Out walked the old fellow to the very edge of the parapet and gazed over. Off flew the arrow and in the twilight it was lost to vision, but he heard it strike and saw the ram wheel in flight. As it disappeared over the ridge Art followed at a run; reaching the top he peered cautiously about and saw the sheep at no great distance standing still with its legs spread wide apart. He knew by the posture that it was done for. So he went back to the valley and because of the distance from camp and the oncoming darkness he made a fire and "Siwashed it" or camped out in the open all night without blankets. In the morning he went after his trophy and found it near the spot last seen. It was a fine specimen. The arrow had pierced it from front to rear completely through and was lost; a center shot at eighty yards; a most remarkable bit of archery and hunting stratagem. This head now decorates the dining room of the Young home in San Francisco. Unfortunately the moose antlers were cached near a river in Alaska and an unprecedented flood carried them out to sea.

While speaking of Alaskan rivers there recurs to my mind a most remarkable incident related by Young. In one picture required for their film it was necessary to show a canoe in the course of construction, the subsequent use of this vessel and an upset in the turbulent waters of the river. To represent his bow in its canvas case, and still to spare that weapon a wetting, Young went down the river bank to pick out a stick about the same size to put in his bow case. Taking the first piece that came to hand he started to place it in the case, when struck by its smoothness he looked at it and found he had a weatherbeaten old Indian bow in his hand. It seemed like a sign, a good omen,—for we playfully indulge in omens in these romantic adventures with the bow.

Studying this implement later I found it apparently to be a birch Urock bow, some five feet long, having nocks and a place for the usual perpendicular piece of wood bound on at the handle to check the string. It would have pulled about sixty pounds, good enough for caribou hunting.

And so in brief are the adventures of Art Young in Alaska.

But who can speak of the adventures in the heart of our archer? Here is no common hunter, no insensate slayer of animals. Here we have the poet afoot,—the archaic adventurer in modern game fields; the champion of fair play and clean sport; all that is strong and manly.

I take off my hat to Arthur Young.

A CHAPTER OF ENCOURAGEMENT
BY
STEWART EDWARD WHITE

No one can read Dr. Pope's book without an appreciation of the romance and charm of the long bow and the broad-head arrow. And no one can doubt that the little group of which he writes has proved that the thing can be done. Its members have brought to bag quantities of small game, unnumbered deer, mountain goat, big horn sheep, moose, caribou, thirteen black bears, six grizzlies, and one monster Kadiak bear. That point it proved beyond doubt. But, each will ask; how about it for me? These men are experts. It all looks very fascinating; but what chance have I?

That, I believe, is the first reaction of the average man after he has savored the real literary charm of this book and begins to consider the practical side of the question. It was my own reaction. Fortunately, I live within commuting distance of Dr. Pope, so I have been able to resolve my doubts—slowly. My purpose is here to summarize what I found out.

In the first place, the utter beginner has in his hands a weapon that is adequate and humane. A bad rifle shot or a bad shotgun shot can and does "slobber" his game by hitting it in the wrong places or with the outer fringe of his pattern. But if an arrow can be landed anywhere in the body it is certain and prompt death. This is not only true of the chest cavity, but of the belly; and every rifleman knows that a bullet in the latter is ineffective and cruel, and a beast so wounded is capable of long distances before it dies. The arrow's deadliness depends not on its shocking power, which of course is low, but upon internal hemorrhage and the very peculiar fact that the admission of air in quantity into any part of the body cavity collapses the lungs. Furthermore, again unlike the bullet, the broad arrow seems to be as effective at the limit of its longest flight as at the nearer ranges. So the amateur bowman, suitably armed, may lay this much of comfort to his soul: if by the grace of Robin Hood and the little capricious gods of luck he does manage to stray a shaft into a beast, it is going to do the trick for him. And of course if he keeps on shooting arrows in the general direction of game, the doctrine of chances will land him sooner or later!

In the meantime—and here is the second point—he is going to have an enormous amount of enjoyment from his "close misses." With firearms a miss is a miss, and catastrophic. You have failed, and that is all there is to it; and you have no earthly means of knowing whether your miss was by the scant quarter inch that fairly ruffled the beast's crest, or by the disgraceful yards of buck ague or the jerking forefinger or the blinking dodging eye. But the beautiful clean flight of the arrow can be followed. And when it passes between the neck and the bend of wing of wild goose; or it buries its head in the damp earth only just below the body line of the unstartled deer, the bowman experiences quite as keen a thrill of satisfaction as follows a good center with gun or rifle,—even though the game is as scathless as though he had missed it by miles. In this type of hunting a miss is emphatically *not* as good as a mile! And the chances are he can try again, and yet again, provided nothing else has occurred to affright his quarry. To most animals the flight of an arrow is little more than the winging past of some strange swift bird.

Thus the joy is not primarily in the size of the bag, nor even in the certainty of the bag, but in the woodcraft and the outguessing, and the world of little things one must notice to get near enough for his shot, and the birds and the breezes and the small matters along the way; which is as it should be: and the satisfaction is not wholly centered in merely a shot well placed and a trophy quickly come by. Indeed, the latter is become almost an incidental; a very welcome and inspiring incidental; a wonderful culmination; but a culmination that is necessary only occasionally as a guerdon of emprise rather than an invariably indispensability, lacking which the whole expedition must be classed as a failure.

At first the seasoned marksman will doubt this. I can only recommend a fair trial. One of the most successful experiences of my sporting life was one of these "close misses." A very noble buck, broadside on, was trotting head up across my front and down a mountain slope nearly a hundred and fifty yards away,—out of reasonable range as archers count distances. I made my calculations as well as I could and loosed a shaft, more in honor of his wide branching antlers than in any sure hope. While the arrow was in the air the deer stopped short and looked at me. The shaft swept down its long curve and shattered its point against a rock at just the right height and about six feet in front of the beast. If he had continued his trot, it would have pierced his heart. Nothing was the worse for that adventure except the broad-head, which was gladly offered to the kindly gods who had so gratifyingly watched for me its straight true flight. And I had just as much satisfaction from the episode as though I had actually slain the deer,—and had had to cut it up and carry it into camp. This would not have been true with a rifle. At any range of the bullet's effectiveness I should have expected of myself a hit, and a miss would have hugely disappointed me with myself and ruined temporarily my otherwise sweet disposition.

But even acknowledging all this, the fact indubitably remains that one must occasionally get results, one must occasionally *expect* to get results, in order to retain interest. Even though one goes forth boldly to slay the bounding roebuck and brings back but the lowly jackrabbit, he must once in a blue moon be assured of the jackrabbit. And he must get the jackrabbit, not merely through the personal interposition of the little gods who preside at roulette tables, but because his bow arm held true and his release sweet and the shaft true sped.

All this is perfectly possible. Any man can within a reasonable time become a reasonably good shot if he has the persistence to practice, and the patience to live through the first discouragements, and the ability to get some fun along the way. The game in its essentials seems to me a good deal like golf. It has a definite technique of a number of definite elements which must coordinate. When that technique is working smoothly results are certain. Like golf a man knows just what he is to do; only he cannot make himself do it! As the idea gets grooved in his brain, the swing—or the release and the hold,—become more and more automatic. But always there will be "on" days when he will shoot a par: and "off" days when both ball and shaft fly on the wings of contrariness.

Of all the qualities above mentioned, I think for the beginner the most important is to cherish confident hope through the early discouragements. For a long time there seems to be no improvement whatever. And there is not improvement as far as score-results go. But the man who studies to perfect the elements of his technique, and is not merely shooting arrows promiscuously, is actually improving for all that. He must strive to remember that not only is each and every point important in itself, but that all must coordinate, must be working well together. No matter how crisp the release, it avails not an the bow arm falter or the back muscles relax. Again like golf, one day one thing will be working well, and another day another; but it is only when they are *all* working well that the ball screams down the fairway or the arrow consistently finds its mark. Thus the beginner, practise as thoughtfully as he may, will for a time, perhaps a month or so, find little or no encouragement in the accuracy of his shaft's flight. This is the period when most men, who have started out enthusiastically enough, give up in disgust. Then all at once the persistent ones will begin to pick up. It is a good deal like dropping stones in a pool. One can drop in a great many stones without altering the surface of the water; but there comes a time when the addition of a single pebble shows results.

In his chapter on Shooting the Bow, Dr. Pope has most adequately outlined the technique. If the beginner will do what the doctor there tells him to do, he will shoot correctly. Nevertheless he will find it necessary to find out for himself just *how* he is going to do these things. It is largely a matter of getting the proper mental picture, and finding out how one feels when he is doing the right thing. Each probably gets an entirely individual mental image. Nevertheless a few hints from the beginner's standpoint may come gracefully from one who only yesterday was a beginner, and who today has struggled but little beyond the first marker post of progress.

The target game and the hunting game differ somewhat, but the actual technique of releasing the arrow is the same in both. I strongly advise the use of a regulation target at regulation distances for at least half of one's practice. There is an inexorable quality about the painted rings. One cannot jolly oneself into a belief of a "pretty good one!" as one does when the roving arrow comes close to the little bush. Those rings are spaced in very definite inches! Even when one has graduated into a fairly hopeful hunting field, one returns every once in a while to the target to check himself up, to find out what he is doing wrong. And in the target, too, one can find the interest along that valley of preliminary discouragement. One should keep all one's scores, no matter how bad they may be. Even if a lowly seventy is the best one has been able to accomplish, there is a certain satisfaction in going after a not-so-slowly seventy-one. Every ten scores or so average up, and see what you have. Thus one can chart a sort of glacial movement upwards otherwise imperceptible to one's sardonic estimate of himself as the World's Champion Dub.

Begin with a light bow; but work up into the heavier weights as rapidly as possible. The first bow I used at target weighed forty pounds. The first hunting bow, made for me by Dr. Pope, weighs sixty-five. I could draw it to the full, but only with difficulty; and it was not in any proper control. I seriously begged the doctor to reduce it for me, alleging that never would I be able to handle it. He very properly laughed at me. Within the year I had worked up to the point where seventy-five pounds seemed about right; and at the present writing I have one of eighty-two pounds that handles for me much easier than Dr. Pope's gift did at first. So begin light, but work up as fast as possible. Do not linger with a weak bow simply because it is easier to draw and because you can with it, and a light target, make a better target score.

Beware of shooting too much just at first. If you strain the muscles of your drawing fingers you will have to lay off just when you are most eager. They strengthen very rapidly if you give them a chance. Once they are hardened to the work you will have no more trouble and can, as far as they are concerned, pop away as long as your bow arm holds out; but if once you get them tender and sore you will be forced to quit until they recover. It's as bad as a sprain.

Start at forty yards. Stand upright, feet about a foot apart, facing a point at right angles to the target. Turn the head sharply to the left and look at the bull's-eye. *Do not thereafter move it by the fraction of an inch.* Bring your right arm across your chest. Pause and visualize the shot, collecting your powers. Now promptly raise your bow in direct line with the target. Draw the arrow to the head as it comes up. All your muscles are, up to this point, alert but tensed only to the extent necessary to draw the shaft. At the exact moment of release, however, they stiffen to the utmost. It is like a little spurt of energy released to speed the arrow on its way. That, I think, is what Dr. Pope means when he says one should "put his heart in the bow." It helps to imagine yourself trying to drive the arrow right through the target. Pay especial attention to the muscles of the small of the back. The least relaxation there means an ill-sped shaft. The bow arm must be on the point of aim, and *held* there. The release must be sharply backward, and vigorous. Personally I find that my mental image is of contracting the latissimus dorsi—the muscles of the broad of the back by the shoulder blades—and thereby expanding the shoulders, forcing the hands apart, but still in direct line with the bull's-eye. And after the arrow has left the bow, *hold the pose!* Carry through! Imagine yourself as a statue of an archer, and stay just in that position until you hear the arrow strike.

Just in the beginning, at forty yards, with thirty arrows, you may be satisfied if you hit the target between sixteen and twenty-one times out of the thirty shots and make a score of from sixty to eighty points. Your ambition will be, as in golf, to "break" a hundred. By the time you have done that your muscles will be in shape and you can begin on the American Round. At first you will probably make a total of about two hundred for the three distances. Progress will show in your averages. They will creep up a few points at a time. It will be a proud day when you "break" three hundred. Eventually you will shoot consistently in the four hundreds; and that is about as far as you will go unless you devote yourself to the target game, and confine yourself to its lighter tackle and the super refinements of its delicate technique.

The bow you will finally use for practice at the target will not be a hunting bow. It will be longer and more whip-ended and not so sturdy. But if you are to get the best results for the hunting field, I believe it should approximate in weight the hunting weapon. It should not be quite as heavy, for one shoots it more continuously. The one I use weighs sixty pounds. With a lighter bow one would probably make a somewhat better score; but that is a different game. Do not get the idea, however, that mere weight is the whole thing. Nothing is worse than to be over-bowed; and many a deer has been slain with a fifty or fifty-five pound weapon. Only, there is a weight that is adapted to you at your best; that "holds you together"; that keeps you on the mark; that calls your concentration; and that is like to be on the heavier rather than the lighter side as judged by beginner's experience.

In conclusion, let me urge you eventually to make your own tackle. Personally, I am not dexterous when it comes to matters of finer handicraft; and when I became interested in this game I made up my mind that the construction of a bow or the building of a decent arrow was outside my line, and that I would not attempt it. After a while Pope persuaded me I ought to try arrows, at least. Under protest I attempted the job. The Doctor says it takes about an hour to make a good arrow. I can add that it takes about four hours to make a bad one. Still, when completed it did look surprisingly like an arrow, and it flew point first. Pope looked it all over and handed it back with the single comment that I certainly had got the shaft straight. But that arrow was very valuable. It proved to me that I could at least follow out the process and produce *some* result. It also convinced me that Ashan Vitu—who was a heathen god of archers—possessed a magic that could make one drop of glue on the shaft become at least one quart on the fingers; and that turkeys are obsessed with small contrary devils who pass at the bird's death into the first six feathers of its wings and there lurk to the confusion of amateur archers. But I wanted to make another arrow; and I did; and it was a better arrow and took less time. I have that first arrow yet. It is a good idea to number the output; and to preserve a sample out of every three dozen or so, just to show not only your progress but also the advance of your ideas as to what constitutes a good arrow. And some you will probably find valuable for especial emergencies. Number Three of my own product is just such a one. It starts straight enough for the point at which it was aimed. When about thirty yards out it begins to entertain its first distrust of its master, and to proceed according to its own ideas. It makes up its mind that it has been held too high, and immediately goes into a nose dive to rectify the fault. Instantly it realizes that it has overdone the matter, and makes a desperate effort to straighten back on its course. A partial success darts it to the right. Number Three becomes ashamed and flustered. Its course from there on is a series of erratic dives and swoops. I should be very sorry to lose Number Three, for I am quite confident that I could never make another such. When my most painstaking shooting has resulted in a series of misses, I launch Number Three. There is no particular good in aiming it, though it can be done if found amusing. But it is surprising how often it will at the last moment pull off one of its erratic swoops—right into the mark! As a compensating device for rotten shooting it is unexcelled. It is a pity to laugh at it as much as we do; for I am convinced it is a conscientious arrow doing its best under natural handicap; like a prima donna with a cleft palate, for instance.

In a manner not dissimilar to my beginning of the fletching art, I took up bow making. It can be done. The only thing is to go at it without any particular hope. Then you will be surprised and pleased that you have achieved any result at all, and will at once see where you could do better again. To make a very fine bow is a real art and requires much experience and many trials. But to make a serviceable bow that will shoot and will hold up for a time is not very difficult. And it is great fun! The first occasion on which you go afield with bow, bowstring, arrow, quiver, bracer, and finger tips all of your own composition, and loose the shaft and the thing not only flies well but straight and far, you will taste a wonder and a satisfaction new to your experience. It will probably take you some time to convince yourself that somehow the whole outfit is not a base imitation.

From that moment you are a true archer, and you will actually look with tolerance on anything so stiff and metallic and mechanical as a gun. Your wife will accustom herself to shavings and scraps of feathers on the rugs. Inspirations will come to you anent better methods, which you will urge enthusiastically on the old timers; and the old timers will smile upon you sweetly and sadly. They had those same inspirations themselves in their green and salad days. Then no longer will you need a Chapter of Encouragement.

THE UPSHOT

In ancient times when archery was practiced in open fields and shooting at butts or clouts, men walked between their distances much as golfers do today, and having completed their course, it was often customary to shoot a return round over the same field. This was called the upshot, and has descended into common parlance, just as many other phrases have which had their origin in the use of the bow and arrow.

So we have come to the end of our story and prepare to say good-bye.

Although we have said much, and probably too much of ourselves, we have not spoken the last word in archery. There are a few things that we have learned of the art; others know more. And though we would praise our pastime beyond measure, protesting that it is healthful, admirable and full of romance, yet we cannot claim that it accomplishes all things and is the only sport a man should pursue.

Its devotees will find ample room for differences of opinion. The shape of a feather and the contour of a bow have been subjects for argument since time immemorial. Nor is our art suited to all men. Few indeed seem fitted for archery or care for it. But that rare soul who finds in its appeal something that satisfies his desire for fair play, historic sentiment, and the call of the open world, will be happy.

People will scoff at him for his "medieval crotchet," will think of him as the Don Quixote of Sherwood Forest, but in their hearts they will have a wistful envy of him; for all men feel the nobility and honorable past of our sport. It carries with it dim memory pictures of spring days, the green woods and the joy of youth.

It is also futile to prophesy the future of the bow and arrow. As an implement of the chase, to us it seems to hold a place unique for fairness. And in the further development of the wild game problem, where apparently large game preserves and refuges will be the order of the day, the bow is a more fitting weapon with which to slay a beast than a gun or any more powerful agent that may be invented.

Of course, there are those who say that all hunting should cease, and that photography and nature study alone should be directed toward wild life. That sweet day may come, but at least no man can consistently decry hunting who eats meat, wears furs or leather, or uses any vestige of animal tissue; for he is party to the crime of animal murder, and murder more brutal and ignoble than that of the chase.

And those who think the bullet is more certain and humane than the arrow have no accurate knowledge on which to base their comparison. Our experience has proved the contrary to be the case.

Yet these are not the reasons why we shoot the bow: we do it because we love it, and this is no reason; it is an emotion difficult to explain.

Nor should I close this chapter without reference to that noble company of archers, the members of the National Archery Association—men and women who can shoot as pretty a shaft as any who ever drew a bowstring. The names of Will Thompson, Louis Maxson, George P. Bryant, Harry Richardson, Dr. Robert P. Elmer, Homer Taylor, Mrs. Howell, and Cynthia Wesson are emblazoned on the annals of archery history for all time. To them and the many other worthy bowmen who have fostered the art in America, we are eternally grateful. The self-imposed discipline of target shooting is much harder work than the carefree effort of hunting. The rewards, however, are less spectacular.

To you who would follow us into the land of Robin Hood, let me say that what you need most is a great longing to come, and perseverance; for if I should try to explain how we have accomplished even that little we have in hunting, I would protest that it is because we have held to an idea and been persistent. In my own mind the credit is ascribed to the fact that I have surrounded myself with good companions and tried again and again in spite of failure.

All that we have done is perfectly possible to any adventurous youth, no matter what his age.

Nor is that which is written here the finis, for even as I scribble we are on our journey to another hunt, and bowmen seem ever to be increasing in numbers.

May the gods grant us all space to carry a sturdy bow and wander through the forest glades to seek the bounding deer; to lie in the deep meadow grasses; to watch the flight of birds; to smell the fragrance of burning leaves; to cast an upward glance at the unobserved beauty of the moon. May they give us strength to draw the string to the cheek, the arrow to the barb and loose the flying shaft, so long as life may last.

Farewell and shoot well!

Made in the USA
San Bernardino, CA
12 December 2016